TRANSFIGURATION

The School of the Prophets

BY

TRANSFIGURATION
The School of the Prophets
Copyright © 2025 by Keira Brinton

All rights reserved. No part of this publication may be reproduced, stored in a retrieval system, or transmitted in any form or by any means, electronic, mechanical, photocopying, recording, or otherwise, without written permission of the publisher or author, except for the use of brief quotations in a book review.

Although the author and publisher have made every effort to ensure that the information in this book was correct at press time, the author and publisher do not assume and hereby disclaim any liability to any party for any loss, damage, or disruption caused by errors or omissions, whether such errors or omissions result from negligence, accident, or any other cause.

Adherence to all applicable laws and regulations, including international, federal, state and local governing professional licensing, business practices, advertising, and all other aspects of doing business in the US, Canada or any other jurisdiction is the sole responsibility of the reader and consumer.

Neither the author nor the publisher assumes any responsibility or liability whatsoever on behalf of the consumer or reader of this material. Any perceived slight of any individual or organization is purely unintentional.

The resources in this book are provided for informational purposes only and should not be used to replace the specialized training and professional judgment of a health care or mental health care professional.

Neither the author nor the publisher can be held responsible for the use of the information provided within this book. Please always consult a trained professional before making any decision regarding treatment of yourself or others.

To request permissions, contact the publisher at
publish@joapublishing.com or contact@keirabrinton.com

Hardcover ISBN: 978-1-967575-36-7
Paperback ISBN: 978-1-967575-35-0
eBook ISBN: 978-1-967575-37-4
Printed in the USA.

Joan of Arc Publishing
Meridian, ID 83646
www.joapublishing.com

A LITTLE GIFT FOR YOU

Thank you for saying yes to this work.
As a heartfelt thank-you, I've created a small bonus just for you:

Create Your Sacred Space (Mini-Course)

This is a simple, step-by-step guide to consecrate a corner of your home for daily communion with God.

Access your gift:
Scan the QR code below:

May this help you carve out a sacred place—where your breath slows, your heart softens, and the frequency of miracles begins to hum within you—so that you may sit at the foot of God and **ask, listen, and do**.

Expect Miracles.
Keira

Transfiguration

Table of Contents

Introduction 1
My Sacred Agreement 3

PART I: Awakening The Call 9
Chapter 1: The School of the Prophets 11
Chapter 2: The Call to Remember 15
Chapter 3: The Path of Becoming 19
Chapter 4: The Pattern of Miracles 23

PART II: Navigating The Challenges 27
Chapter 5: When Doubt Follows Vision 29
Chapter 6: Burn Without Breaking: The Surrender of the Called .. 38
Chapter 7: The Ancient Pattern You Are Walking 48
Chapter 8: The Loneliness of the Prophet 56
Chapter 9: The Doorway: *Standing at the Threshold* 67
Chapter 10: Where Is God? 71
Chapter 11: The Call, the Fear, and the Fallout 80
Chapter 12: The Reward of the Called 96

PART III: The Laws of Transfiguration 101
Chapter 13: God Is a Magnifier & Multiplier 103

Chapter 14: The Currancy of Miracles 110
Chapter 15: Trust, Doubt, and the Language of Faith 115
Chapter 16: The Edge 122
Chapter 17: Where Power Meets the Wound 126

PART IV: The Practice 131
Chapter 18: May We Prepare to Sit at the Foot of God 133
Chapter 19: The Sacred Centers 143
Chapter 20: The Sacred Submission and the Washing of Mercy . 150
Chapter 21: Re-coding Your Cells 157
Chapter 22: DNA Transfiguration 164

PART V: Living As A Prophet 171
Chapter 23: Learning to Live after Transfiguration 173
Chapter 24: The Persecution of the Prophets, and,
Disrupt Anyway 177
Chapter 25: Live as the Prophet Now 183

ADDENDUM: Blessings from the Prayer Corner 189
I. Daily Entry Blessings 191
    The Fast Version of the Blessing: 191
    The Blessing of the Body: 192
II. Transfiguration Blessings 199
    The Full Transfiguration Blessing: 199
III. Identity & Calling Blessings 209
    Blessing of the Prophetess 209
    Blessing of Self-Love 212
    I Am Loved Blessing 217
IV. Abundance & Divine Mother Blessings 226
    Blessing with the Divine Mother around Abundance 226

Introduction

Each morning I roll out of bed and stumble through my dimly lit room to my prayer corner—a corner that has been dedicated, consecrated, and prepared for the communion with God.

On the ground lies my beautiful, white fur rug, and lain gently on top of this rug is my gold and cream prayer mat.

A white porcelain pitcher filled with water stands at the head of my prayer mat. Cradled at its base is a baby-blue, imperfect bowl I found in a humble pottery shop during a sacred journey to Japan with my sons.

I quietly sit down, place my teal prayer shawl—that is detailed with golden beads—over my head in reverence, and pour fresh water from the pitcher into the bowl.

I ask that Christ bless the walls, the floors, the doors, and everything in my room so that it will be cleansed and activated to match the frequency of miracles. I then ask that Christ touch the water so that it will be cleaned and activated down to the molecular structure so that it will match the structure of miracles.

I do this to make it sacred.

Transfiguration

I dip two of my fingers into the water and anoint different parts of my body, blessing each chakra with the energy of miracles. After I have blessed my crown, third eye, eyes, ears, nose, lips, throat, heart, solar plexus, sacral, root, hands, and feet, I sit in the newness of the energy of God.

I then ask that God, the Divine Mother, and Christ will place their hands on my head to give me a blessing. I ask that I may receive the words that I need to hear that day.

And then I pick up my well-loved, leather-brown prayer book and place my pen on the pages.

As I do this . . .

Words are given to me.
Words I do not know.
Concepts I couldn't have even imagined.

And I am taught.

This is my school.
This is my worship.
This is my church.

Every morning, I meet with God.

And . . .

Every morning, God teaches me.
Every morning, I renew the covenant I made years before writing this book.

My Sacred Agreement

On February 17th, the floodgates broke. Memories of my childhood abuse surged to the surface, not in fragments but in a relentless storm. It struck like a wave that capsized my soul, leaving me buried beneath a heaviness almost too much to bear. And because of this, it seemed the only way out was to die. As I considered taking my life, I felt a presence appear in the room. And I knew it was God. I could not see God, but I knew without a doubt it was God.

And I felt these words pulse through me:

—

"You have work to do. You need to stay."

—

As those words moved through me, it was as if my cells were being reorganized and rewritten.

It was a death, not of the physical form but of the spiritual. My old self died in that moment, and from the ashes of that darkness emerged a leader I could not have imagined. This command from God seemed to be a magnet to my truest self—the one who had been called before she arrived on this earth but had been hidden for most of my life.

Transfiguration

She was the one who made the covenant. Not the broken 34-year-old Keira but a version that was strong, powerful, and clear.

I felt this covenant rise from within the depths of me. A covenant that stated that **IF I WAS** to stay . . . I would do whatever God asks of me.

And I have kept that covenant.

It has been in the keeping of such a contract that I have witnessed miracles upon miracles occur. This book itself is one of the many invitations God has given me since that day.

And while I have been blessed to witness God move mountains, part my very own Red Seas, and pour down miracles like manna, it has not been easy. And still, vision after vision has been given to me and then birthed right before my eyes, all while I've been raising five kids as a single mother, moving through fear, loneliness, and burnout.

I have lived a million lives in my 42 years. And though so much of my world has burned, again and again, one constant has remained.

And that is God.

God has never left. Even when I felt like He had . . . I now can clearly see the fingerprints left on everything in my life. *The fingerprints of God.*

And that is why I write this book.

I write . . . because my life is devoted to God. I have given everything I have in service to God. And in return . . . God has walked with me.

I'll refer to God as "Him" throughout the book—this is simply the way my heart learned to speak to this Higher Presence. Even so, God is beyond any word or pronoun. I use the word "God" because it feels most familiar, though it will always be smaller than the Reality I know.

My Sacred Agreement

As you read, please know that the way you commune with the Divine is exactly right for you. Use the language that resonates in your soul.

Whether you say God, Universe, Spirit, Allah, Yahweh, Elohim, Father, Divine Mother, or another name entirely, this book is here to remind you of one thing . . .

You have access to this Supreme Being.

YOU.

You do not need to be perfect or holy to hear, commune with, and receive from on High.

You do not need to go through anyone or any religion to meet with God.

This book will teach you that **YOU** are the conduit and you are received just **AS you ARE**.

I believe that you are here because you have been called, anointed, and chosen.

You are gifted.
And because of this, you might not fit with the masses.

You most likely have tried to run away from your gifts, your callings, and your uniqueness.

But God has called you, and until you claim your callings, stand in your anointing, and **CHOOSE YOUR** path . . . life can be a struggle.

My hope is that as you read this book, you will see the path of others who have been called, just as you have. You will find yourself in their stories, and by doing so, you **WILL** claim your calling and rise as the leader you were chosen to be.

Transfiguration

My calling is to be the prophetess God has called me to be.

I am here to gather the prophets and prophetesses of this time—to remind you of who you are and the work you have been called to do, to write, and to **BE**.

I am here to remind you that you, too, have been called, and that there is a formula that will help you transfigure **INTO** the fullness of your calling, so you can live and breathe miracles into the world . . . now.

I wrote this book to gather all religions, all spirituality, all humans together under the Presence of the All-knowing Being, God.

One morning in my daily blessing from God, these words were given to me:

—

Teach people how to be transfigured, and they will be the conductor of miracles.
They have to stop waiting to be saved.
They have to stop worshipping their struggles.
They have to embody their own strength and alchemize the pain into gold.
They are the miracle workers.
Help people take responsibility for their lives.
They are the stewards of their lives. They hold the power to create miracles.
They just need to understand how to be with God.

—

Which is what this book is designed to do.

My Sacred Agreement

I have prayed over the words on these pages. I have blessed them to find those who have been called, and to aid in the transfiguration of the humans who are meant to lead.

May this book be the beginning of the **School of the Prophets** here on the earth. A guide for all who desire to hear God, walk with God, speak and write the words that will lead others to do the same.

I now give this book over to God in sacred surrender.
I have done my work. May God now do what God would do with it.

Expect Miracles.
Keira

Transfiguration

PART I

AWAKENING THE CALL

Transfiguration

> For those who have been called are being awakened now. Awakened to their gifts, awakened to their visions and to their own unique path.
>
> Devotion is the action they take.
> Faith is the language they speak.
>
> And miracles are the frequency in which they are held.

CHAPTER 1

The School of the Prophets

Welcome to the School of the Prophets.

The doors are opened. The path has been paved by many before us. Seraphim of light are ready to take the coal from the altar of the most High to cleanse and prepare our mouths so that you may meet with God and speak His words into the world.

Now is the time. The time to soften our hearts so that we may receive, clear out our ears so that we may hear God, and prepare our feet so that we may stand in truth and claim the Sacred once again.

I have been called, just as you have. I know we are not the only ones. The heavens are open, and many are being called.

The time has come for many prophets and prophetesses to rise, to claim their roles in the expansion of light, and to honor the God who has called them to do so.

There were many prophets in ancient times. They lived in different cities and on different continents. They were leaders.

Transfiguration

They were rebels. They were disruptors. They did not conform. They did not follow the masses. They were seekers.

It was devotion, not perfection, that made them prophets.

They were called by God. They answered that call. They sat in stillness and reverence. They received Divine messages. They wrote these messages into books. They also spoke them into the hearts of humans.

These collective prophets changed the trajectory of the world. As they obeyed God's call, they transformed lives.

And so it is with you.

I believe that a prophet or prophetess is one who receives a call, a vision, and a knowing from God. They devote their time, their energy, and their focus to ask, listen, and do.

In times of old, the prophets asked. They heard. They saw. And . . . they received.

They carried what God taught them, writing those sacred messages into books. From towering walls and steps, they lifted their voices. They did not receive inspiration and then remain silent. They received, and they declared.

This marked the path of the prophet.

Their stories were different from each other, but their paths were similar.

The time of prophets is not dead.

Now is the time for MANY to rise up and claim their role as this leader. It is time for a new wave of prophets and prophetesses to rise.

The earth has long felt the absence of such power and wisdom, **but now is the moment.**

Those who are called and anointed must step out of hiding to be seen and heard. It is time to transfigure into the ones who will birth the visions God has entrusted to them and claim their rightful place as leaders.

Be the ones who walk with God and help others do the same.

You are not average. You are rare. You may have tried to outrun your gifts, your voice, your knowing, but the truth remains: **you are chosen.**

And until you stand in your anointing, life may feel like a struggle. The struggle comes because your soul has already agreed to this mighty work. When you live beneath it, nothing feels right. Even the wind against your skin can sting. Relationships may feel like battlegrounds, jobs like prisons of stagnation and monotony.

Until you rise in your gifts, your life remains only half-lived.

And you, my love, were not meant to live a life half-lived.

You were made to lead.
To hear from God.
To deliver messages that shift nations, families, and futures.

The world is waiting.

The world is waiting for you.

This book is for you.

The prophet.
The prophetess.

Transfiguration

The miracle worker.
The one who walks with God.

And so from the deepest place of gratitude within me I say . . .

Welcome to the School of the Prophets.

CHAPTER 2

The Call to Remember

May we remember.
Remember who we are, remember our callings, and remember God.

Remembrance is not new information. It is a journey to what your soul already knows.

In my remembering, God brought me to the stories of the prophets to help me return. I was led into the ancient accounts to learn the gifts of faith and inspired action. There I witnessed the Law of Transfiguration—a quickening available not only to Moses but to all of us.

In those moments, God asked me to write this book—an invitation to uncover the Law of Transfiguration.

God didn't choose me to write this book because I already understood this law; He chose me because I didn't. It is in our unknowing that God often calls those with open hearts, so He can teach His truths without prior assumptions clouding His voice. In such soil, miracles take root.

Transfiguration

Many prophets were illiterate for this reason: God chooses those who desire but don't yet understand, so they can be true vessels, receiving without their opinions drowning out the voice of God.

I was asked, and so I am now here to receive.

I want you to know that I do not write this book as a scholar. I write it as a religious dropout, a rebel, a disruptor—but mostly, I write it as a seeker.

For me, writing this book mirrors the scripture:
"precept upon precept; line upon line . . ." Isaiah 28:10 (King James Version)

This means that I am not shown it all at once, but slowly, line upon line, as I write. Whenever I sit in prayer, the next step is shown; whenever I touch the keyboard, the words are given.

And so, I am learning the Law of Transfiguration as I write this book.

I invite you to join me.

Join me in the inquiry.

Meet me in this quest if you are hungry: hungry for more light, more expansion, more wonder, more faith, **MORE MIRACLES** . . . simply hungry for **MORE**.

If your soul feels as if it is finally getting its thirst quenched with this very thought, then stay.

Stay and drink. *Stay and swim.*

For these waters are deep, and as we seek . . . may we never thirst again.

The Call to Remember

When you choose to step into waters like these, time begins to soften. No matter where you are, as you read this book, you and I will step outside of time. The words on these pages will open pathways that lead us to where our feet match the stride of those who came before us.

May we turn our heads and see Moses beside us. May we look down and see Christ's feet walking with us.

As we read these words, we will walk with Moses, walk with Christ, walk with the prophets of old, and we will sit at the foot of God.

This book will be a bridge. It will take us to where we need to go to receive what we have been seeking.

Let these words rewrite the patterns within your cells. Allow them to awaken the songs of remembrance within you.

I invite you to linger in the moments your soul begs you to stay. I invite you to go deeper with God—especially in the places you most want to avoid.

But most of all, I call forth your higher self—the one who knows God, the one who has been called, the one who walks with light, breathes with light, and creates with light.

And from that place of remembrance, I offer you the blessing God gave me:

—

Remember. Remember. Remember.

For it isn't that you need to know. It is simply a call to remember, for it is imprinted on your very cells.

Transfiguration

Untether your mind from today and the now, and ask to unlock the memories of your cells, so that the wisdom of the Greats might be given to you.

Breathe with them, for they lived under the same moon and stars as you do. They were made of the same bones and flesh.

Call them to walk with you—to tell you the stories that will activate the memories of old.

There is no beginning or end. There is only the solidification of remembrance.

—

This book won't be new information for you. It will be a journey of remembering.

You already know the Law of Transfiguration. You already know the energy of quickening. You have everything you need to call forth any miracle you desire.

It's just time to remember.

The messages within these pages are a remembrance to your soul.

The invitation is simple: quiet the mind, soften your heart, and breathe deep into the truth that **YOU DO KNOW**.

And now let us walk with the Greats.

The ones who can call this forth from the very cells that live within you.

Let us unlock the miracles we are here to awaken as we quicken our beings in the fire of transfiguration.

CHAPTER 3

The Path of Becoming

To walk with God is to walk a path of becoming, a path that asks for your whole self, not just the light you already trust but the shadows you have tried to outrun.

This journey is not passive. It is transformational, cellular, demanding, and sacred.

And if we are to invite your highest light to lead, we must acknowledge the parts of you that also know the dark, because darkness is part of this path.

Without it, there is no light.

Trees die without the resistance of wind pushing against them. Likewise, light only shines when it contrasts with darkness. And the more light you carry, the more darkness you have faced.

The darkness is part of the recipe.

Just as cookies need flour—without it butter, sugar, and eggs melt into a sweet puddle that never sets—so darkness is the binding ingredient of transfiguration. It is required. You cannot become without it.

Transfiguration

Wholeness is forged through the union of light and dark. Let each teach you; let each shape you.

When you have been a student of them both, you cannot return to the old self, to the slavery of normalcy and stagnation. And it is right here, in this union of opposites, that the next phase of the journey begins.

Light and dark are the co-contributors to creation, and creation is the only path that can now hold you. For creation is what calls us into BEING a leader.

Creation is what unites us with God. Creation is the thread that aligns us with our callings. And creation itself begins with a question.

Divine creation invites us to ask, listen, and do.

As you ask, listen, and do, you have the opportunity to become quickened. For what we are being asked to create and bring to this earth requires a new energy, a quickened energy: the energy of becoming.

Quickening is a fierce fire of love, transformation, and acclamation to the light of God. This is what we need to bring God's visions to life. It is what strengthens us when our visions feel too overwhelming.

I know that the visions you have been receiving may seem far too big for you to comprehend, bigger than you could ever imagine. I understand that you might not know how to birth them. But when we learn how to quicken our energy to match these visions, the visions unfold.

And this I know: when we ask, we will receive.

This law is woven through every ancient story. If we ASK, we will RECEIVE. Just as gravity is a law, so is this promise. It is written in every holy text, over and over again, because it is so.

The Path of Becoming

"Ask and it will be given to you; seek and you will find; knock and the door will be opened to you. For everyone who asks receives..."
Matthew 7:7-8 (NIV)

"Ask, and it will be given to you; seek, and you will find; knock, and the door will be opened to you."
Luke 11:9 (NIV)

"Ask, and it shall be given unto you; seek, and ye shall find; knock, and it shall be opened unto you."
3 Nephi 14:7 (The Book of Mormon)

"If any of you lacks wisdom, you should ask God ... and it will be given to you."
James 1:5 *(NIV)

If you ask, you will receive. And as you become, you will arrive.

The arrival is not a location or destination. It is a deep level of confidence, confidence that this law will be honored, that when you ask, God will speak.

Whoever you are, when you ask, *God will answer*.

You will find this truth layered through the stories of the ancient prophets. These ancient stories are like honey to my soul. They bring me peace and trust. These stories teach us what we need to understand.

They are parables that allow our minds to more deeply comprehend the higher principles of God. These stories bypass the conscious mind and move directly into the subconscious mind, the mind that speaks to God and allows us to bend time, weave miracles, and build worlds.

There will be moments on this path when the pressure feels like it might break you, moments where the intensity of what God is asking

Transfiguration

you to carry feels like compression, a tightening, a narrowing, a fire that threatens to consume you.

This is not a sign you are failing. It is the precursor to transfiguration.

Every time a new vision arrives, it will stretch you. It will press against the edges of who you have been until you expand to match what God is placing in your hands. The compression leads to the transfiguration.

And as you continue to walk, the path will keep unfolding. The river of miracles will carry you to the next piece of land. The next right step will arrive just in time.

As long as you ask, listen, and do, even when fear rises, even when the requirements feel unreasonable, miracles will move through you, around you, and beneath your feet.

This is how you will know that God still speaks to humans, because you will hear God.

You will ask.
You will listen.
Fear will rise.
And then you will become.

You will unshackle the chains of fear and live by the same ancient anthem carried by prophets, seekers, and leaders throughout time:

I will go and do as God commands.
Ask, and you shall receive.

CHAPTER 4

The Pattern of Miracles

The path you're on is not new. It has already been trodden, worn smooth by the feet of many.

And as you begin to recognize the divine rhythm beneath your life, you will see the pattern of miracles that has always been waiting for you. When this awareness awakens, the impossible becomes possible.

Visions will be given, and miracles will be required.

Visions are almost always too great for our own eyes. They stretch us. They terrify us. They ask us to become someone new. And when we share them with those whose hearts have been guarded by pain, those who cannot bear such magnitude, they often try to dismantle what God has given, not out of malice but because they cannot see how such a thing could ever be done.

This is how visions die, trampled beneath the weight of another's fear.

This is what Christ meant when He taught, "Cast not your pearls before swine." Matthew 7:6

Transfiguration

Your visions are the pearls. Sacred. Holy. Not meant to be scattered for approval.

For visions are meant to be impossible. It is through the impossible that we become who God is shaping us to be. And it is in the becoming that we step into the ancient rhythm, the pattern of miracles that every prophet before us has walked.

One morning, as I sat in my prayer corner with tear-stained cheeks and a heart exhausted from yet another insurmountable task, I told God I was tired of big problems. I was exhausted from carrying what felt too heavy for one person to hold.

And God answered with a truth so clear it pierced through my ache:

—

Big problems are the key to the door that opens to miracles.
You cannot have miracles without big problems.

—

The moment those words entered me, peace followed. Suddenly, everything made sense.

The pressure was great because the miracle that was coming was great. The impossibility was not proof of abandonment; it was the precursor to provision.

And with that knowing, a thread became visible to me, the pattern woven through every miracle God had ever shown me.

This pattern had been teaching me long before I ever recognized it, especially through the stories of Moses. His life has been one of my greatest teachers, not through formal study but through revelation. God has shown me his stories so vividly, so repeatedly, that they feel less like scripture and more like remembering.

The Currency of Miracles

I have stood with him at the edge of the Red Sea where the impossible was delivered in faith. I have watched the waters rise into walls, watched a nation walk through on dry ground, watched the terror and relief collide in their lungs as freedom opened before them.

And I have stood in that very place myself, staring into situations that had no earthly way forward, only to watch the waters part when faith became my only path.

I have tasted manna in my own life, financial provision appearing in the exact moment of need, again and again. I have known the temptation to hoard out of fear, and I have seen how quickly miracles spoil when fear becomes our master. I have felt the humanness of it, the part of me that wants certainty even while living inside the supernatural.

And just as Israel longed for freedom and yet mourned for slavery, I, too, have watched myself long for the past when the future felt too big.

I have seen God ask something as simple as looking at the staff, an act so small it seems absurd, and yet life depended on that single act of faith. I have seen myself struggle with that same simplicity, resisting what God asks because it feels too ordinary to matter.

And I have knelt, like Moses, hungry to understand what God is doing, sobbing under the weight of the visions I've been given, feeling the ache of leadership and the blessing of obedience all at once. In those moments, I learned what Moses learned: that quickening happens the moment we say yes, and provision follows the moment faith moves.

Through every scene, every revelation, every echo of his life within mine, I have come to understand something profound.

These are not just ancient stories.
They are mirrors.

Transfiguration

They are patterns.
They are the rhythm of the miraculous.

And they are playing out in your life as surely as they have played out in mine.

This is why you feel pressure. This is why the path feels uncharted. This is why the instructions feel impossibly large.

You are walking where others have walked. You are stepping into a rhythm older than time.

You are not alone. Not now. Not ever.

The prophets before you placed their feet one step at a time, guided by a melody of faith that did not die when they did. That melody still sings beneath the surface of your life, urging you forward, shaping your becoming, calling you into a frequency where miracles are not exceptions but inevitabilities.

If you let yourself feel it, if you breathe with them, walk beside them, let their courage awaken the ancient memory within you, you will realize something sacred.

You are a prophet, as they were.
You have walked them.
You have heard God before.
You have known this path since long before you arrived on it again.

And when big problems arrive, you can know with certainty: God is placing a key in your hand.

A miracle is forming.
A miracle bigger than anything you have yet imagined.

This is the pattern of miracles.

And now, it is your turn to walk it.

PART II
NAVIGATING THE CHALLENGES

Transfiguration

The path of the prophet is not for the weak.
Even though, at times, **you will feel weak.**
Even though your knees will shake, and your heart will ache, and you will wonder if you have been mistaken.

The truth is: You are among the strongest.
Your path is simply harder—
Not because you are being punished, but because you are being prepared.
The weight you carry is not to crush you.
It is to build the sacred muscles that will steward miracles.

The challenges you face are not barriers.
They are invitations.
They are forging your gifts.
Deepening your faith.
Sharpening your sight.

Your path has been plagued by loneliness and hardship, mostly because no one told you that it was *always* supposed to start that way.
But when you begin to understand that you are walking a path well-tread by prophets before you—
When you realize that you are not lost, not abandoned, not failing—

When you realize that this is how your path was meant to be . . .
Then, **you rise differently.**
You walk with a fierceness anchored in faith.
You move with the fire of the anointed.

CHAPTER 5

When Doubt Follows Vision

We are told that Moses had to be transfigured to sit with God. But I do not believe that. I believe: Moses did not have to become something first before God would sit with him. God was already there, ready and waiting for Moses.

You do not have to BE worthy for God to sit with you. You do not have to be perfect to receive. No . . . you do not need to be transfigured to sit at the foot of God.

You must become transfigured to BE as God. To call forth the miracles WITH God.

And the transfiguration? It occurred WHEN GOD called Moses. The transfiguration was activated BECAUSE the vision and calling were so BIG, it required Moses to BECOME different.

He wasn't changed because of who he was in that moment: an exiled prince, stripped of status, wandering the desert as a shepherd. He was changed because of who he was called to be.

Transfiguration

The transfiguration happened the moment God told him he would free an entire civilization. Moses was transformed by that vision. It happened the moment he agreed to SEE himself AS God saw him.

And this is the moment where doubt begins its ancient dance with destiny. Because as soon as the calling arrives, the shadows rise.

When we wipe the sleep from our eyes and choose to see as God sees . . .
When we take the cotton from our ears and hear as God hears . . .
When we step into the vision God has already placed in our palms . . .
When we choose to become the ones who can claim miracles . . .

Doubt will always try to meet us there.

It rises like an old nightmare, an echo of the past trying to pull us back into smallness. This is the pattern threaded through every prophetic story ever told. It was true for Moses. It is true for you.

When God called Moses, he resisted. He questioned. He doubted. He said the words so many of us have whispered on bathroom floors, in dark nights, or in quiet moments when the vision felt too big:

"Who am I?"
Exodus 3:11 (NIV)
"Who am I that I should go to Pharaoh and bring the Israelites out of Egypt?"

Every time God has called me into my next big vision, I find myself on my knees asking, "Who am I to do THIS, God?" And perhaps . . . you've asked the same.

When Doubt Follows Vision

Every leader I've helped write a sacred book, build an inspired business, or step into miraculous visions has said some version of this same phrase: "Who am I to do this?"

It is here, right in the opening breath of a calling, where the illusions rush in. Memories of failures. Memories of rejection. Memories of limitations handed down through lineage and experience.

They swirl and tighten, forming the first lies: "I'm not qualified." "I'm not ready." "I'm not good enough."

But these aren't warnings. They are trailmarkers, signposts that you've stepped onto holy ground. They signal that the path ahead will require a greater reliance on God than you have ever known.

When Moses voiced his fears aloud, God didn't comfort him with flattery or qualifications. God simply said:

"I will be with you."
Exodus 3:12 (NIV)

God didn't call Moses because of his strengths. God called Moses because of his willingness. And God didn't call you because you were ready. He called you because you are willing.

If you don't feel qualified, that is not a disqualifier; it is confirmation. It means you are moldable. It means you are a seeker. It means you will lean into God, and that is the very posture required for miracles.

And yet . . . self-doubt is never the final test. It is simply the first trembling at the edge of a greater becoming.

Because once you question yourself, the next illusion rises like a shadow behind it, not about who you are but about how others will see you.

Transfiguration

Moses voiced it next:

"What if they do not believe me or listen to me?"
Exodus 4:1 (NIV)

So God took what Moses already had, a staff—something simple, ordinary, unimpressive—and turned it into a conduit of divine power.

God never asked Moses to produce the miracle. He asked Moses to show up. God would do the rest.

The same is true for you. You need only bring what you have, and God will multiply it.

When doubt grips tightly, there is only one place to take it: into the presence of God.

I remember crawling into my prayer corner, draping my shawl over my head, and whispering with the last breath of belief, "God . . . help me release this doubt."

And God answered:

—

Trust.
For each day the sun rises, and each night the stars appear.
There is a rhythm of the universe at play.
Seek first, but then allow.
The stars will guide you.
Trust that I have a master plan for you.

—

Another morning, when doubt roared loud enough to drown out truth, God offered a firm, holy reprimand to me:

When Doubt Follows Vision

—

May you rest in the hope.
May you find surety in the trust.
May you rejoice in the beauty.
How dare you ever doubt?
You have seen your own Red Sea part.
You have watched miracles rain down from the heavens.
Do not doubt, for that is what is holding My promises from you.
Doubt is not your god.
Stop worshiping it.

—

Doubt exists only so trust can deepen. Without doubt, faith would have no weight.

And so God shows us the vision in pieces. If God had told Moses every step from the beginning—the desert, the plagues, the Red Sea swelling at his feet, the chariots thundering behind him—if Moses had seen all of it in one moment, he may have fainted beneath the weight of it.

So God gave him only what he could hold. One direction at a time. One breath at a time. One miracle at a time.

One morning, God showed me exactly why:

—

The maze may seem overwhelming and claustrophobic from inside.
But from above, it is a beautiful shape to look at.
Stop being in the maze.
Look at it from above, and wonder.
Stop wandering, and wonder.

—

Transfiguration

And in this, I saw myself: lost in human perspective, clinging to the ground view. Forgetting God sees the entire map from above.

He doesn't ask us to chart the course. He asks us to follow the visions given to us.

Yet, even when direction is clear, weakness can make us hesitate. Moses had a weakness. He stuttered. Yet, he was the chosen messenger.

This was God's point. Moses's weakest place became the exact portal for God's strength.

When Moses cried:

"I am slow of speech and tongue."
Exodus 4:10 (NIV)

God responded:

"Who gave human beings their mouths? . . . Is it not I, the Lord?"
Exodus 4:11 (NIV)

You were never expected to carry your calling through your own strength. You were only invited to say yes.

Even after reassurance, Moses tried one more time:

"Please send someone else."
Exodus 4:13 (NIV)

And who hasn't said that? Who hasn't felt that?

But Moses was not alone in this resistance. Gideon hid. Jeremiah protested. Jonah ran.

Even Jesus, in Gethsemane, asked for another way:

"If You are willing, take this cup from Me; yet not My will, but Yours be done."
Luke 22:42 (NIV)

Even the Son of God felt the weight of His calling. But unlike the others, Jesus did not run. He did not resist. He felt the weight of it . . . and said *yes*.

Yes is the turning point. *Yes* is the activation. *Yes* is the moment miracles begin.

God does not need you fearless. He does not need you ready. He does not need your skills perfected. God needs your *yes*.

And once you give Him that yes, He will meet you with miracles. He is a God of magnification, but He cannot magnify what you refuse to move on.

If Moses had stayed in the desert, Israel would have stayed in chains. The Red Sea would never have opened. The covenant would not have unfolded.

But fear and doubt can rise loud enough to take your faith-filled yes and tilt it into a no.

So before you close your eyes to the visions God has placed within you, before you plug your ears to the words that pierce your soul from the Divine, you must understand the cost.

When you refuse your calling, there are two costs. The first cost is what the world loses. The second cost is what you lose.

When you ignore your calling, when you turn your eyes to the ground while the light is beckoning you forward, the world loses out on the gift you and God were meant to bring forth together.

Transfiguration

Your calling isn't meant to sit dormant inside you. It was given to move through you, to make waves, to change lives, to bring truth to the places where illusion has cocooned the mind.

If you step back, shrink down, or silence yourself, the world loses the very miracle God intended to deliver through you.

And you lose something too.

Ignoring the call creates a spiritual unrest that cannot be medicated or bypassed: depression, agitation, stagnation, the ache of unrealized purpose, a holy ache that grows louder with every "not now" you whisper to God.

Jonah felt that ache deep in the belly of a whale, a darkness of his own refusal. Peter felt it in the piercing cry of a rooster, a sound that shattered him awake to the truth of who he was called to be.

The cost of refusing the call is too high.

But Moses didn't run. Moses said yes. Even in fear. Even in doubt. Even in uncertainty.

And because of that *yes*, he became a leader whose obedience split seas.

You have been called too.

How do I know?

Because these words found you.

And the moment you say yes, the moment you agree to see yourself as God sees you, your transfiguration begins.

So the question now rises like a holy echo. Will you step into your vision? Or will you bear the cost and watch the world bear it with you?

When Doubt Follows Vision

The cost of not moving is far too great.

Your calling is here. Your doubt is not your enemy; it is simply the place where your faith sharpens.

Now we walk.

Now we rise.

Now we move into the fire that forges the called and prepares the path for the becoming.

CHAPTER 6

Burn Without Breaking: The Surrender of the Called

Early one morning as I sat in prayer, I asked God for my daily blessing and these are the words I was given . . .

—

Fierceness is freedom.
Anything else is not worth doing.

—

And so I offer these words to you now.

Let them land.

Let them burn. Let them forge the fire inside you that cannot be extinguished. May this section awaken the fierceness that lives deep in your soul. May it tear down the lies that say you are weak. May it call you boldly into the destiny you chose before you came here.

This is the place where you no longer just hope for miracles. This is where you become the miracle.

Burn Without Breaking: The Surrender of the Called

You do not walk forward by sight. You walk forward by the fire of faith. And it is HERE where you claim, with boldness, the callings God has given you.

This fire is meant to awaken your gifts, your passion, and your purpose. But many do not speak of the shadow this fire can bring.

You were meant to burn with the fire of your vision. But if you try to control it, if you grip it like it's yours to manage, the fire that burns within you will burn you instead. And you will feel as if you are going to break.

That's why this fire was never meant to be carried alone. And for some reason, we feel as if we are meant to carry it all on our own, like it is our role and responsibility to hold the world on our shoulders.

I know what it feels like to have said yes to God without knowing how it would all work out. I feel the weight of your heart right now. I feel your exhaustion wrapped in obedience, the fire of purpose mixed with the ache of depletion.

And I just want to remind you that you are not failing. You are being forged.

Fire is the only element that can melt metal, destroy cities, and yet at the same time, warm cold bodies and cook food for nourishment. This is the fire we must go through to become the leader that we have been anointed to be.

The fire that feels as though it will consume you is only here to burn off the old and prepare you for the new. You are being called to the edge, not to fall but to become the version of yourself who will no longer need to carry it all.

You have said yes at every turn. You have obeyed even without a safety net. You have followed divine inspiration into uncharted,

Transfiguration

expensive, unknown, and expansive territory . . . because you were called.

And possibly the cost of this path has felt that it has taken you: taken your energy, your joy, your finances, maybe even your passion. The vision that pulled you to this path can sometimes feel as if it is a lost treasure and a faded memory.

But it is in these moments when you crawl into your prayer corner, battered and tired, singed from the very fire that you started, and whisper these words . . .

"God . . . can You please take care of me too?"

This is not a selfish request. It is a holy surrender. Palms up, heart softened, and a plea that must be met. A plea that pulls God to your prayer corner like a magnet to metal. A prayer that doesn't beckon but demands.

And it is here where the fire that seems to have burned you simmers, and the diamond that God has been forging you into starts to sparkle.

It sparkles when you unclasp your fists and ask for God to guide you—guide you every minute, every second of this day—where you lay down your fears and the need to carry it all on your own and finally rest INTO God.

You're tired because you weren't meant to carry the weight of the divine vision all by yourself.

This is the moment where you say to God:

"If You called me to this, then You must fund it.
I will keep showing up—but I need You to show up too."

"I am no longer available to run myself into the ground for my purpose."

"I choose to be provided for, not just used as a vessel."

This is the turning point where you and God become partners.

You are a vessel, but you are not a martyr. You are a channel of the Divine, but you are also loved by God, known by God, and you're allowed to place sacred boundaries, even with God.

You can say:
"I will carry the vision—but I need You to carry me."
"I am willing to pour out—but I must also be poured into."
"I am available for the mission—but not at the expense of my
nervous system, my body, or my peace."

This isn't rebellion.

This is a true partnership. And I believe God is waiting for you to speak such boundaries. God is inviting you to step up and PARTNER in this work.

This is what it means to be a vessel without being consumed. Just like the bush that burned but was not destroyed, but instead was used as a sign and a symbol of God's presence on earth, so are you being lit.

You will not be consumed by the fire within, for when you partner with God in your agency and boundaries, you become that bush that burns with fire. You become it to be a testament that God is real, that God does exist, and you will shine with the light of this higher truth.

You were never meant to burn alone. God is just waiting for you to lay down the world you keep picking up and carrying on your own.

Transfiguration

But you must remember that this is not a one-time experience. You don't just lay down your burdens once and walk freely for the rest of your life.

Because even when we know we are not supposed to carry it all, we still try. We keep going. And in the going, we will forget God. Not on purpose but out of habit.

Our muscles have grown stronger so we can actually carry more weight, and in that strength, the remembrance of giving it all to God will slip from our minds. We will pretend that we are fine, until suddenly—we're not.

The calling will grow too heavy. And once again we will fall to our knees, crawl into our prayer corners, and wonder how we forgot . . . again.

But this is not because you were weak.

It is simply because your vision was too heavy. Because the thing God asked you to carry felt bigger than your body, like trying to breathe underwater, like being asked to fly without wings.

And it is in these moments that the vision that once felt holy begins to feel like torment. This is when the dream turns into a burden.

It is here, where you feel you have been pushed to the very edges of your skin, feeling like God has asked you to become something impossible. It is here, where the fire burns hotter than ever before.

And in that moment, the one where you fear you will never escape this immense heat, the one where you fear you will not survive . . .

In THAT moment.

This is when you become.

Burn Without Breaking: The Surrender of the Called

I want you to not only read these words but let them be written in the very belly of your heart.

You were chosen. And so you have what you need.

Your gifts were designed specifically for this calling. But your gifts lay dormant until they hit the fire. It is here that they are sculpted into the tools needed to do the work God has prepared for you.

Do not turn away. Instead, sit in the warmth. Allow God to refine you, and then as you peel back your tightly clasped fingers and open your palms to God, laying down the world you so desperately believe you are meant to hold on your own, the fire will slowly die.

Peace will arise like a newly sprouted flower. And you will step forward with a deeper surety, a strength that abides all storms, and the clarity of vision will arrive.

You will see what many cannot see. For those who choose to meet God in the fire become.

It was on a day such as this, where I found myself broken, burned, and exhausted, that God spoke these words to me in the early morning of my dark prayer corner:

—

Marvelous are the works of God. Miracles are the breath of God. No prophet has done this on their own.

The seas wouldn't have parted.
The dead would never rise.
The sick would not have healed.
This cannot be done alone.

—

Transfiguration

Partner with God every second, and you will find the freedom you seek.

True partnership arrives not before the fire, *but in it.*

You are not alone in this story: the story of being called, being forged, wanting to quit, and somehow still rising to the task that has been given to you.

Hannah was a heroine of the Old Testament. She was barren, heartbroken, and completely exhausted. And in the deepest ache of her calling, which was to become a mother, she went to the temple and wept bitterly.

She cried so deeply that Eli, the high priest, thought she was drunk. But she wasn't drunk. She was broken.

Her grief didn't look holy, but it was. She was crying out from the deepest ache of obedience. She pleaded to God:

"And she vowed a vow, and said, O LORD of hosts, if thou wilt indeed look on the affliction of thine handmaid, and remember me, and not forget thine handmaid, but wilt give unto thine handmaid a man child, then I will give him unto the LORD all the days of his life, and there shall no razor come upon his head."
1 Samuel 1:11

How many times have you felt crazy for wanting what God placed on your heart?

Let me remind you that you're not crazy. You're willing.

You are one of the few still willing to believe that God speaks to humans. You are a courageous soul who is willing to believe in visions. You are brave enough to dream and believe that miracles are real.

Burn Without Breaking: The Surrender of the Called

You are known by God, and your visions bring you to your knees so that you may become one with God.

And then there's Moses, the man who saw God face to face, the one who parted the Red Sea, called down plagues, carried the holy tablets, and led a nation. And still, he broke.

Not because he didn't believe in the promise. Not because he wasn't faithful. But because the calling wore him down. The pressure became too much.

And so one day, Moses cried out:

"I cannot carry all these people by myself;
the burden is too heavy for me.
If this is how You are going to treat me,
please go ahead and kill me."
Numbers 11:14–15 (NIV)

When we think of Moses, we rarely think of this story. Yet, this moment happened.

And do you know how God responded? Not with punishment. Not with judgment. Not with. "Be a better leader."

God said:

"Gather for me seventy of Israel's elders . . .
I will take some of the spirit that is on you and put it on them.
They will share the burden of the people with
you so that you will not have to carry it alone."
Numbers 11:16–17 (NIV, NRSV)

God allowed Moses to feel held and seen, and He sent help to hold the weight. Because even Moses was never meant to carry it all alone.

Transfiguration

So let me ask you now: Have you been holding your vision like it's your job to make it all work? Have you been trying to "figure it out" instead of giving it over? Have you forgotten that the God who gave you the vision is the only One who can sustain it?

Trying to carry your vision alone is like trying to build a house without a blueprint. God is the designer. God is the builder. God is the architect.

You are the vessel and the channel. You are the one who said yes.

But why are you holding this as if it's your job to make it all work?

You're not supposed to carry it alone.

The moment you stop gripping the vision like it's yours to fulfill, the moment you plead in prayer, "God, take it," it is here where the heavens open.

Let your words become your agreement. And let this be the moment you say yes to divine relief.

Take a nice deep breath in, one that fills you to the edges of your lungs. As you breathe out, feel the peace that only arrives when a weight has been lifted, and then speak these words out loud:

"God, I ask to partner with you. I see this vision, I love this vision. And while I am willing to carry it, I will not carry it alone."

I choose rest. I choose ease.
I choose partnership.
I choose to be funded, held, and poured into.
I trust You to open the heavens.
I release the weight.
And I make room for the miracle."

Remember . . . God did not call you to lead alone. God does not expect you to move the mountains on your own.

No. God called you to partner in this vision.

Ask and you will receive.

CHAPTER 7

The Ancient Pattern You Are Walking

I know what it feels like to live a life that is different than any you have ever seen before. It may feel as if you are walking on a path that has never seen footprints. But that is simply not true.

The path has already been walked, lived, proven, and carved into the fabric of time. The leaders who have come before us have softened this road that we now tread. They have prepared it with their own tears, their own feet, and their own knees that knelt deep in prayer.

It is an illusion to believe that we are the first to step foot here, for there were many who have prepped this path for you.

And among every prophet God has shown me, among every ancient story that has woven itself into my cells, there is one whose footsteps I have followed more times than I can count: Moses.

Not because I studied and memorized his scriptures, but because God revealed his life to me so vividly, so repeatedly, so intimately, that it has felt less like learning and more like remembering. I was not there

The Ancient Pattern You Are Walking

in the desert, yet God has shown me those scenes in such detail I might as well have stood among the Israelites myself.

I have been taken into his story again and again, not to observe it but to experience it. And as God revealed Moses's life to me, I came to understand that these ancient stories were not meant to just be read. They were meant to be lived.

Because the pattern he walked is the same pattern you are walking now.

I have stood with Moses at the edge of the Red Sea. I have felt the impossibility of that moment, the terror of the waves, the thunder of chariots behind us, the icy bite of fear that screams from the depths of aching lungs, "God . . . there is no way out. How did you bring me here, only to leave me caged in?"

And I have seen God lift the impossible in one, single breath. I watched the waters rise like towering walls. I watched the ocean split clean in two. I watched the pathway of deliverance appear where, moments before, there was only death.

I stood there like a silent bystander, watching the children of Israel carry their little ones through the waters ON dry ground. I saw them, and then I saw me. For I have lived that moment in my own life, standing at my own Red Seas that should have drowned me, watching God part them in ways I could never have imagined.

This is the pattern of God: stand where escape seems impossible, and watch a new possibility be born. It is here that we must surrender it all. Surrender our minds, our paths, our solutions and allow—allow for God to part the Red Sea of our life. This is what God taught me as I stood beside Moses.

But that is not where this journey ended.

Transfiguration

God then placed me next to the children of Israel as they walked through the wilderness. I saw them cry in hunger. I felt their fear rise like the water they had just conquered. I saw the joy they felt when the first day of manna appeared. Sweet, nourishing food that fell from the sky like rain, but didn't dissipate into air, yet, instead fed their starving bodies.

I saw God drop birds at their feet, so that they could be fed from their meat. And then I would witness it—the fear would win over their gratitude. It would come in like a dark plague eating away at their hearts and whispering words into the backs of their minds.

Words that said, "God provided today . . . but how do you know He will provide tomorrow?"
"It was better to be a slave. You knew that everyday there would be food. How do you know there will be food tomorrow?"
"God led you here with miracles. But He has left. You are all alone with no map to guide you."
"Hurry, stuff your pockets with manna. You must, because you have a family to feed."

I saw these whispers edge into the corners of their minds, just as simple thoughts. But soon these thoughts infiltrated the camp. Fear was no longer a suggestion; it became the idol they worshiped.

As God carried me through these past memories, *I was shown that I was no better.*

I saw the moments where I tasted manna. Not theoretical manna. Not symbolic manna. Real-life, real-time manna.

My manna didn't appear in the form of sweet food from the sky. Instead, my manna arrived in the form of provisions that appeared in the exact moment of need. They were never early, never late, and always perfect.

The Ancient Pattern You Are Walking

Three times in a single year, God placed $200,000 in my hands within twenty-four hours of my deep prayers, all to keep my business alive. Manna would arrive when it seemed as though all provisions were gone. Each time these moments defied logic, planning, and man-made timelines.

It was my manna. Pure, miraculous manna.

And yet, just like the children of Israel, I've also been the one who woke up the next morning and panicked. In that panic, I would then hoard what God gave me, simply out of fear. More times than I count, I have clenched the blessing that God granted me because I was afraid it wouldn't come again.

And just like the manna of old, what I tried to protect in fear, the miracle would spoil in my hands.

At first I thought God was punishing me because I had fallen back into my old patterns of fear. But God wasn't punishing me. The miracle I received was never meant to be stored in fear. It was meant to be multiplied by faith and fueled by trust.

Fear spoils while faith multiplies.

The more I would trust that God would send manna, right on time, the provisions would arrive. The more I let faith fill my being, my mind, and my words, the manna would continue to appear.

But these trips back to the time of Moses weren't complete.

God then placed me in the crowd: the crowd of the mothers, the fathers, and the children as they walked through the wilderness. Forty years of walking. And I walked beside them and heard the children of Israel complain against Moses.

Transfiguration

They were longing for slavery even after witnessing their deliverance. EVEN after they had prayed for freedom, they ached for their prisons. They wanted slavery because slavery doesn't require faith. Slavery doesn't need a God. Slavery is the familiar they weren't willing to compromise.

As I walked beside them, I saw myself. I saw the times that I longed for old patterns, not because they were sacred, but because they were familiar. I knew the muscles that were needed in those patterns. Even when they didn't serve me, they seemed to feel like an old friend.

And so even after God would part my own Red Sea, I would cry to go back: back to fear, back to abuse, back to suffering.

As I would witness their weakness, and then I would see mine, it was so simple as I watched them. Through the children of Israel, I saw it.

Freedom feels frightening when you have lived most of your life in captivity. And freedom comes at a cost.

You must be willing to see the truth. You must ask to SEE as God sees. And you must empty your pockets and let the fear and doubt empty out. Then cup your hands and place them at the corners of your heart and allow faith to drop in.

Breath in the faith like the fresh ocean breeze or the mountain air. Let faith soak deep into the marrow of your bones. *And then lift your foot and keep walking.*

God cannot create miracles if you choose to stand still.

Sometimes, the visions God gives us are far too great for our comprehension. And then there are times when God asks something of us that feels too easy, so easy we brush it off and ignore it.

The Ancient Pattern You Are Walking

I was shown this as I was taken back to the time when Moses asked the children of Israel to look at the bronze serpent on his staff. And with this one simple action, they would be saved. And yet, many did not look.

Not because it was hard, but because it was so easy they didn't believe.

The miracle required nothing but a glance. Faith was the only requirement. And still, many chose to not look, and they died.

I have felt that same resistance in myself, resisting what God asks not because it is difficult, but because it feels too small to matter.

I have found this pattern to be true for me:
Small acts = Big miracles.
Tiny obedience = Infinite return.

God doesn't always need us to part the Red Sea.

You don't always need to be traveling across a wilderness. The miracles live in the tiny actions that are driven by inspiration. And each small action compounds upon another, resulting in a life not only filled with miracles but the life you were always called to live.

And then there are moments when you feel as if you might crack under the pressure of such enormous visions, the steps ahead feeling like you are sinking in quicksand with concrete on your shoulders.

I saw myself when God took me to the moment where Moses felt this. I knelt beside Moses as he buried his face in his hands, trembling under the weight of leadership. I have felt his exhaustion, his confusion, his fear, his heartbreak for the very people he was called to lead.

I have knelt in that posture too, the posture of the prophet: broken, surrendered, obedient, unsure.

Transfiguration

I know that moment so well, the one where I wept through my tears and said, "God, I will go where You send me . . . but please, strengthen me for this road." Just as Moses did, so have I. Just as Moses did, I am sure, so have you.

All of these trips back to the time of Moses, always appearing as I continue to move forward with my calling, could never have prepared me for the moment I saw Moses at the burning bush.

I saw clearly that the story I had been told was not the story I now witnessed.

Moses did not have to be holy to be transfigured. No, the calling God was giving him was so mighty it transfigured him. He was not changed because he was qualified. He was changed because God asked something that required him to become more than he had ever been.

You are being asked the same.

This is why your calling feels impossible. This is why the pressure feels unbearable. This is why your nervous system trembles. This is why your bones feel like they are being rearranged. This is why your old identity cannot hold.

God is not breaking you. God is building you. And the blueprint is the story of Moses.

I do not believe that these stories are distant myths. They are mirrors. They are showing you who you are. They are showing you what is possible. They are showing you what God does with those who say yes.

Because you, too, are a prophet. You, too, have been called. You, too, are standing at your own Red Sea with chariots closing in behind you. You, too, are being asked to believe for manna before you see it fall.

The Ancient Pattern You Are Walking

You, too, are being asked to lift your eyes to stare at the staff and trust that even the most simple inspired actions will free you.

You, too, are being asked to lead yourself into freedom that scares you.

You are walking in ancient footsteps. You are walking with ancient fire.

And when the pressure feels too great, when the vision feels too heavy, when the call feels too large for your lungs, know this: you are walking the very same pattern that delivered nations, parted seas, raised leaders, and brought miracles into the world.

You are not alone. Not for a moment. Not for a breath. Not for a step.

This is the pattern of miracles.

And now, it is being written through you.

CHAPTER 8

The Loneliness of the Prophet

Prophets are often profoundly alone. The deeper the anointing, the heavier the isolation. The more intimate your walk with God, the more alien you may feel to the world. The deeper your obedience, the more silence you must often sit in.

The prophet's path is not paved with applause. It is carved in solitude. It is refined in private, and in the places no one sees.

The path is held together by conversations with God that no one else hears.

No one tells you this when you say yes to God. But every great prophets and prophetess of the past has felt this.

Moses went up the mountain alone to meet God and came back with Divine knowedge—only to find the people were afraid of his light. Jesus asked His closest friends to stay awake with Him, and they fell asleep. He wept blood in Gethsemane—completelty alone—before

The Loneliness of the Prophet

His greatest calling. At the end of His earthly mission, we even read of Jesus uttering:

"My God, why hast Thou forsaken me?"
Matthew 27:46 (KJV)

You are not the only one who has felt this way. You are not the only one who has prayed, *"Why me?"* You are not the only one who has wondered why obedience feels so much like abandonment.

But I want you to hear me when I say this: you are not abandoned. You are anointed.

And the loneliness you feel is an echo of those who came before you. It's the sound of the prophets. The ones who stood in their gifts, their differences, and kept walking even when the path ahead was not paved. The ones who carried God's voice when no one else could hear it.

You are not forsaken. And you are never alone.

This is simply a road that is often not taken. To be a prophet means you are in the world but not OF it. It is a sacrifice to walk this path, and yet it will fill you far more than anything the world has ever had to offer.

One morning, when my loneliness was particularly heavy, I went into my prayer corner and this was the blessing I received:

—

The Tower of Babel was built because they refused to build the real tower—the one inside of themselves.
I changed their language not out of punishment but as a gift.
With no one on the outside to speak to, they would need to go within to reach Me.

Transfiguration

This was their cave.
For most of your life, no one spoke your language, and it was for this purpose.
This made you build your own inner tower.

—

At that moment, my whole life began to make sense. I began to see that everything had been for my good. That my language was not the language of those around me, so I would resort to the only One who spoke my innate language, which was God.

But part of this loneliness isn't just about being alone on the path. It's about not being seen or heard for who we truly are. Even Jesus wasn't received in His own hometown. And we—the prophets, prophetesses, visionaries, messengers—are often not seen for the fullness of who we are by the very people closest to us: family, friends, community, those we love most.

This can make us feel crazy. *Crazy and lonely.*

Because all we want is to be seen. To be heard. To have our revelations, our ideas, our sacred downloads be heard for the truth that lives within them.

We want to know that what we're learning is also helping others. We want to serve. We were born to serve. And that desire—so pure, so holy—is what makes the loneliness ache even deeper. Because when the message we carry feels unseen, the purpose can feel crushed. When the love we want to give has nowhere to land, the calling can feel like a burden.

While loneliness is the path, it is also one of the prophet's most dangerous places, not just because it aches, but because of that ache, we often let unvetted people into our life. People who feel like relief but bring ruin. People who entered the sacred when our gates were open out of desperation, not discernment.

We must not let loneliness lead us into distraction, or worse, destruction.

There are many times in this loneliness we wonder if God has called us and then left us. Because this path is one many do not tread, we can find ourselves questioning the very God who led us here. This runs true through many of the stories through holy texts. If we look, we can find holy examples of the lonely path of the prophet.

Samson

We see the power and the danger of loneliness revealed in the story of Samson. Samson was a prophet and judge of Israel, consecrated from birth. His strength was legendary, a divine gift meant to protect and deliver a nation. Yet, alongside that anointing lived deep isolation. He longed to be known beyond his calling, to be loved apart from the weight of his assignment.

And it was here, where loneliness split him open, that Samson let Delilah in. He didn't let her in because she proved to be trustworthy, but because the ache for connection outweighed his discernment. In his desperation to be seen, he revealed what was sacred. He invited a stranger into his inner world, and it was there that betrayal took root.

His hair was cut. His eyes were gouged out. His strength was taken from him. The fall did not come from an enemy advancing; it came from misplaced trust born of loneliness.

As God has revealed the lives of the prophets to me, again and again I see this pattern: loneliness is not just an emotion; it is a vulnerability.

Transfiguration

When left unattended, it distorts discernment and tempts us to hand over what is holy to someone who cannot hold it.

Lesson: When loneliness goes unmet, it can lead us to offer our sacred gifts to hands that were never meant to receive them.
Reminder: God longs to meet you in your loneliness. Invite Him into your longing before you invite another. He will strengthen your discernment and bring the right people to walk beside you, those who honor what God has entrusted to you.
Judges 16 (Bible)

Corianton

We see the destructive power of loneliness revealed again in another prophetic story. Corianton, the son of Alma the Younger, was called to be a missionary. But, in the midst of his sacred assignment, he abandoned the work to pursue the harlot Isabel. His choices weakened the mission, disrupted the work of God, and brought profound grief to his father.

Loneliness and immaturity led Corianton to seek comfort outside his calling, when the very power and stability he needed were already available within it.

Sometimes we invite people into our lives not because they are meant to walk with us, but because the silence feels unbearable. Other times, we press forward with discipline and devotion, doing everything "right," only to discover we are standing alone in a vast interior wilderness, unseen, unheard, and wondering if anyone knows where we are.

As God has revealed the lives of the prophets to me, again and again I see this pattern: Loneliness is not just a feeling—it is a strategy, a lie and a lure designed to pull us away from our callings. Left unattended, loneliness corrupts truth. It distorts discernment. It awakens cravings that feel urgent and endless.

And in those moments of weakness, we find ourselves in the cave, reaching for companionship, validation, or relief from someone who has not been chosen, nor prepared, to walk beside us on this path.

Lesson:
When we allow loneliness to pull us off the path, we may find ourselves submerged in a sea of grief—not only our own but also the grief of those connected to our calling.
Reminder: God does not abandon us in our loneliness. He is faithful to bring the right people to walk beside us at the right time. And in the waiting, God Himself will meet us, filling what feels empty within us, so we no longer seek outside ourselves what He longs to restore.
Alma 39 (Book of Mormon)

Moses

We see another expression of loneliness revealed through the story of Moses. Moses was called through a burning bush and anointed to deliver the Israelites from slavery. He spoke with God face-to-face and was entrusted with divine instruction meant to shape a people in covenant with Him. Yet, his calling was marked by profound isolation.

While Moses was on the mountain receiving the law, clear, explicit teachings about who God was, and how the people were to live, those entrusted to steward with Moses broke their faith and their trust with him. Aaron, his own brother and the high priest, led the people in creating a golden calf, directly contradicting what God had revealed to Moses and commanded him to teach.

It was not merely disobedience. It was a betrayal of trust.

Transfiguration

Later, even after this rupture, Aaron and Miriam spoke against Moses out of jealousy. Though surrounded by people, Moses stood alone in responsibility, carrying both the weight of divine instruction and the grief of being misunderstood by those closest to him.

Eventually, the burden became too heavy.
"I am not able to bear all this people alone, because it is too heavy for me."
Numbers 11:14 (KJV)

Moses didn't run into the arms of someone else. Moses went and spoke his truth to God. This was not a failure of faith but the cost of carrying a calling without adequate support.

And here we see a deeper truth: loneliness does not always lead us into temptation or misalignment. Sometimes, it leads us into greater isolation, where the burden increases, the distance widens, and the calling must be carried with fewer companions than before.

God did not rebuke Moses for this confession. Instead, He responded with provision by calling others to share the burden, distributing the weight, and restoring Moses through the community that God brought forward.

Lesson: Loneliness can arise when sacred trust is broken, leaving the leader to carry both the calling and the consequences alone.
Reminder: God does not ask you to endure isolation indefinitely. Bring the weight to Him. He will respond with support, shared strength, and the people required to sustain what He has called you to carry.
Exodus, Numbers, Deuteronomy (Bible)

Moroni

We see another expression of loneliness through the life of Moroni. Moroni was the final prophet of the Nephites. He watched the complete destruction of his people, their cities, their families, their way of life erased before his eyes. His father was killed. His nation was gone. He lived alone, hiding, wandering, carrying the weight of an ending no one else survived to witness.

Yet, even in isolation, Moroni was entrusted with something sacred: the preservation of the record. He became the sole guardian of a message meant for generations he would never meet.

He writes with devastating clarity:

"And my father hath also was killed by them, and I even remain alone to write the sad tale of the destruction of my people.
But behold, they are gone, and I fulfil the commandment of my father. And whether they will slay me, I know not.
Therefore I will write and hide up the records in the earth; and whither I go it mattereth not."

Mormon 8:3-4 (The Book of Mormon)

Moroni did not betray the sacred because no one was left to witness it. He did not abandon the work because survival was uncertain. He fulfilled the commandment. He wrote. He hid the records. He remained faithful, even when his own future no longer mattered to him.

Loneliness did not lead Moroni into temptation or misalignment. It led him into complete solitude, and there, he chose obedience to the very end.

Lesson: Even in the most excruciating loneliness, we can remain faithful to the message we were born to protect.

Transfiguration

Reminder: God sees what you carry in secret. What feels unseen now may become a lifeline for generations yet to come.
Mormon 8 (The Book of Mormon)

Jesus

And finally, we see this loneliness revealed, even in the life of Jesus.

In His deepest hour of anguish, Jesus did not choose to be alone. He asked not once, but three times. He asked His disciples to stay awake, to watch, to pray, to stand guard while He met with God. And three times, they fell asleep.

This was not indifference; it was their human limitation.

And Jesus did not respond with anger. He did not grow bitter. He did not withdraw His love. Instead, He accepted what was being revealed to Him: that this part of the calling would be carried without human support.

He saw their weakness and still loved them. He recognized the solitude and still stepped forward. Crushed beneath the weight of obedience, Jesus did not abandon the work He had agreed to do. He moved forward with courage, compassion, and complete surrender to the will of God.

Not hardened.
Not resentful.
But resolute in love.

Lesson: Even when you ask, people may not be able to show up. But bitterness is not the path—*love is*.
Reminder: God is with you now, always, and forever. Even when your calling feels like the end, it is unfolding into something far greater than

you could ever imagine.
Matthew 26, Mark 14 (Bible)

If you have felt alone, or even carried shame for letting the wrong people into your heart, into your world, into the sacred, may these stories bring you a sense of grace.

Grace for your path.
Grace for your ache.
Grace for your learning.

You are not alone.

You belong to the same story as the great prophets you've read about. It's as much your story as it is theirs.

When you see and accept this, you have a new choice. You don't have to live in loneliness. You don't have to feel its ache forever.

You can gather with the rest of us. Gather and share. Gather and serve. Gather and remember that we were never meant to do this alone.

Allow yourself to unite with God. Then ask for help in gathering. Ask God to send others like you.

And then take action. Speak. Invite. Open.

We have surpassed the era of the one holy prophet. There are many who are called. They are out there right now, feeling just as alone as you have.

It's time for us to stop walking alone. It's time to stop fearing that we're crazy for seeing the truth.

We can gather hands and call out like children on the playground: *"Red Rover, Red Rover . . . send them all over."*

Transfiguration

Send over the ones who hear the call.
Send over the ones who feel this fire.
Send over the ones who feel as though they are alone.
Send over the ones who are us.

And together, may we build up the walls of fortification around one another. Walls made not of stone but of presence, of power, of knowing.

May we find safety in our brilliance.
May we know we are held by those who can actually hold us.

Because yes, the prophet's path is lonely.
But it doesn't have to stay that way.
Not anymore.

CHAPTER 9

The Doorway: *Standing at the Threshold*

If you have been called, there comes a moment when understanding is no longer enough.

This is that moment.

This is not a full chapter.
It is an intermission.

A pause to let what you have already read settle into your body. A moment to notice what has shifted, what has softened, what has begun to move.

Nothing new is being asked of you here.

Instead . . . a space to breathe, to pause and BE.

If you feel a quiet pull forward, that is not curiosity. *It is readiness.* When you turn the page, you are not learning something new.

You are entering the next phase of the path.

Transfiguration

Take a breath.
Then step through.

If you have received visions that have not yet come to fruition, this chapter is a turning point. Up until now, remembering has been enough. Understanding has been enough. Seeing the pattern has been enough. From here forward, *it will not be.*

This is the moment you shift from visionary to leader.

The moment you stop waiting for permission. The moment you stop trying to calculate every detail. The moment you step out of your own way so God can move through you.

We tell ourselves we are waiting for clarity, but if God showed you the whole picture right now, would you truly move forward? Or would your human mind panic beneath the weight of it?

God does not reveal the full path because the vision is too vast to be held all at once. It is revealed one step at a time. This is not a flaw in the design. It is the design.

Do not wait to see the entire vision before you act. Leadership does not begin with certainty. It *begins with trust.*

Below are messages that God gave me in my prayer corner that pulled me into this pocket of rest, trust, and then inspired action.

—

The maze may seem overwhelming and claustrophobic from inside.
But from above, it is a beautiful shape to look at.
Stop being in the maze.
Look at it from above and wonder.
Stop wandering—and wonder.

Your task is not to solve the maze. Your task is to take the next step you have been given.

Ask.
Move.
Ask again.

That is the rhythm of the Called.

—

I know every corner of your path.
I am guiding you.
Trust Me.
A straight path numbs the mind.
A path with many turns engages it.
This is all for you.

The path you are on was never meant to feel normal. It was meant to wake you up.

The great lie is this: *If I could just see the whole picture, then I would move.*

The path of the Called is not one of understanding. It is one of courage.

Sometimes, the ground only appears once your foot leaves the edge.

—

The mouse that lives in the closet, afraid of the hole, stays caged. But the mouse that ventures out gets the whole world.

You do not need to see the whole path. You only need to take the next faithful step.

—

Transfiguration

I know that at times this path can feel like a maze, tight and disorienting, as if you cannot see where it is leading. I know there are moments when you feel caged by uncertainty, afraid to move because you cannot yet see the whole picture.

These messages are not here to rush you or demand more from you. They are here to remind you that nothing has gone wrong.

God is inviting you to lift your line of sight, to soften your grip on needing to understand, and to trust what is already guiding you.

You are not being asked to solve the maze, only to take the next step. You are not being asked to see the entire path, only to move with courage when the door opens.

This is not recklessness; it is faith in motion.

And this moment . . . *right here*—is the crossing.

This is the doorway. This is the threshold where you stop waiting to feel ready and begin walking as the leader you have already been called to be. **Now.**

CHAPTER 10

Where Is God?

For every miracle I have witnessed, there have also been nights, deep in the dark corners of my life, when I have pleaded, screamed, and cried out loud, *"God, where are You?"*

I have read the scriptures that promise God will never leave or abandon me. And yet, there have been seasons when the heavens fell silent, when God felt less like a living presence and more like an idea I was trying desperately to remember.

In those moments, I questioned everything: my calling, my visions, the actions I had taken in faith that somehow still led me here, alone, with my line to God feeling completely disconnected.

And in that silence, the questions did not arrive gently. They came heavy and unrelenting. *Did I misunderstand God? Did I imagine this calling? Did obedience really lead me here?*

When the voice I had learned to trust went quiet, doubt did not whisper. It pressed in, demanding answers where none were given.

And if you are here now, reading these words, it is likely because you have felt this too. The silence. The confusion. The ache of wondering

Transfiguration

whether God is still near, or whether you somehow lost the connection along the way.

In those moments, it feels like confusion. It's not a loss of faith, *but a loss of signal.*

You keep showing up. You keep praying. You keep listening. And still, nothing answers back. The practices that once anchored you feel hollow in your hands, and the certainty that once steadied your steps feels suddenly out of reach.

And the longer the silence stretches, the more personal it becomes. What once felt like a moment now feels like a pattern. You begin to wonder not only where God is but why He would go quiet now, after you said yes, after your obedience, and after the risk you have taken.

The calling didn't disappear, but the inspiration did. And carrying something sacred without feeling the presence of God can feel heavier than never having been called at all.

And it is here, right in this place, that we discover we are not the first to feel this.

Jesus entered this exact silence, not after failure, not after disobedience but after full surrender.

In the Garden of Gethsemane, He went to meet with God, and the heavens did not answer. He prayed. He pleaded. He asked for another way. And still, the silence remained.

Later, from the cross itself, Jesus cried out the question that echoes through every soul who has ever waited for God to respond:

"My God, my God, why hast thou forsaken me?"
Matthew 27:46 (KJV)

Even Jesus felt the absence. Even Jesus experienced the silence. Even Jesus asked where God had gone.

And yet, God had not left.

What if the same is happening for us?

So often, we grow angry when God is quiet. But anger builds walls, and walls block the very voice we long to hear. What if, in the moments we feel most alone, we are actually being invited into a deeper truth?

What if divine silence is not absence but the space where transfiguration begins?

What if the silence is not something to escape but something that has always been part of the way—a holy interval where the old self falls quiet so something truer can emerge?

In my own walk with God, this has proven itself over and over again. There have been moments that I looked down and could see only my feet on the path, moments when I was carrying an empire God had asked me to carry and suddenly felt the full weight of it on my shoulders.

It was in those moments that the silence began to work on me. The silence led me into surrender—slow, sacred surrender—where something in me loosened its grip and allowed God to do what only He could do.

For in those seasons, the ones when the heavens felt silent, something unexpected unfolded.

In the absence of God's voice, my heart softened. My ears grew more attuned. What initially felt like deprivation became an invitation to go

Transfiguration

into a deeper willingness to listen, to seek, and to stay present instead of pulling away.

This is the pattern. *A sacred one.*

When we are willing to see it, the silence becomes hallowed ground instead of an isolated captivity.

And I have not been the only one to feel this.

This same silence has echoed through history, rising from prisons and wildernesses, from cold stone walls and forgotten places, where many prophets have lifted their eyes and asked the very same question.

This is the pattern of silence.

Joseph

Centuries after Christ, Joseph Smith would find himself in Liberty Jail, cold, starving, betrayed by friends, watching his people suffer while heaven remained silent. From that darkness, he cried out, not in disbelief but in desperation born of obedience:

"O God, where art thou? And where is the pavilion that covereth thy hiding place?"
Doctrine & Covenants 121:1

And God answered him with power:

"My son, peace be unto thy soul; thine adversity and thine afflictions shall be but a small moment."
Doctrine &Covenants 121:7

God was not absent. He was holding space for Joseph to become more than he could have become any other way.

David

We see this pattern again in the life of David. David had already been called. He had already been anointed by the prophet Samuel. He had already been told he would be king. God had chosen him. And still he was running, still hiding in caves, still being hunted by Saul, still living like a fugitive, even though the oil had already been poured over his head and the promise spoken out loud.

He carried the calling, but the life that matched it hadn't arrived. And the waiting wore him down.

This is where we find David in Psalm 13, not posturing, not preaching, but crying out:

"How long, O Lord? Will You forget me forever?
How long will You hide Your face from me?"
Psalm 13:1 (NRSV)

David wasn't questioning whether God was real. He was questioning whether God was still near.

Because when you've said yes, when you've felt the anointing settle on your life, when the vision has burned itself into your bones and you're still in the cave—that's when the silence feels like your very breath has been stolen.

The waiting hurts. The silence is painful. The feeling of being unseen by God, especially after everything you've given, feels like a wound that will never heal.

It's the ache of delay, the ache of invisibility, the ache of wondering whether the promise somehow slipped past you while you were trying to survive.

But this wasn't wasted time.

Transfiguration

David wasn't being hidden. He was being shaped.

The caves taught him how to listen, and the danger taught him restraint. The loneliness he experienced taught him how to turn toward God instead of turning away.

His tears didn't disappear; they turned into songs. His desperation didn't harden him; it deepened him. And over time, slowly, painfully, *his waiting became wisdom.*

David asked, *"God, where are You?"* But he didn't stop with that question, because somewhere in the asking, he returned to trust.

David's life reminds us of something important: that even those who have been called will feel forgotten. Even the anointed will ache. Even the chosen will question.

And still God will always show up.

We see this in the life of Job as well.

Job

Job was righteous and walked uprightly. He honored God. He did everything right.

And still he lost everything: his wealth, his health, his children. Everything.

And in the middle of that devastation, he said what so many of us have whispered through our tears:

"Oh, that I knew where I might find Him..."
Job 23:3 (NRSV)

He wasn't just grieving the loss of every piece of his life. He was grieving what felt like the absence of God *in the middle of the storm.*

Where Is God?

The silence is as equal to the suffering of the storms.

You cry out. You fast. You pray. *And still the heavens feel silent.* And it is here that you wonder if you've been abandoned by the God you serve.

That was Job.

He didn't understand the silence. He didn't know what God was doing behind the scenes. He just knew the pain.

But here's what we learn from Job's story: God was never gone. He was listening and present the entire time.

And when God finally spoke, it wasn't a gentle whisper; it was a whirlwind.

God didn't give Job explanations. He reminded Job of who He was: the Creator, the Sustainer, the One who laid the foundations of the earth.

Job's suffering didn't end because he understood, **it ended because he surrendered.** He let go of needing all the answers. And by doing so he stepped into awe and peace.

And in that surrender, everything was restored.

Double.

This is the pattern of silence.

You lose. You cry out. You feel forgotten. But if you stay close, even in the dark you will be restored.

I believe that these stories tell the pattern of the Divine Silence before Transfiguration.

Transfiguration

Jesus in the garden.
Joseph in the prison.
David in the wilderness.
Job in the storm.

Each of these moments felt like abandonment for the prophet. And yet, they were actually moments of Divine Transformation.

What if the silence is not God's absence but God preparing us to see in a new way? What if the very moment we think God has disappeared is the moment He is calling us deeper, closer?

The invitation is simply *what will you do in the silence?*

Because if Jesus, in His darkest hour, could cry out, "My God, why have You forsaken me," surely we will sometimes ask the same.

And in those moments, we have a choice: We can turn away, believing the lie that we are alone. Or we can lean in, knowing that even when we cannot feel God, He is still near and is preparing us.

The silence is never abandonment. The silence is where the transfiguration begins.

It is here that we are gifted the opportunity to change our cells and the patterns that have been woven so deep within us.

The pattern of being abandoned. The pattern of having to do everything on our own. The patterns of fear and doubt that rise in these moments of silence.

The lack of God's voice deafening within our very ears is where we get to choose differently. It is here that sacred surrender becomes the air we breathe and where we can take our faith and ask God to multiply it.

It is here that we prepare our bodies to meet with God, *again and again and again.*

I have met with God many times, even when I didn't want to. I have met with Him, even when I was angry with Him. I have sat deep in prayer, even when the heavens were silent.

I continued to prepare my body to sit at the foot of God. I continued asking to receive the next step, asking for new visions: visions of WHO I REALLY WAS, visions of what God had called me to do.

And I have been taught that THIS is where the transfiguration is invoked.

Transfiguration doesn't come when everything is working. It doesn't happen when the bank account is full and our lives are smooth as butter. Transfiguration comes when our brokenness demands faith, when the silence moves us to inspired action.

Metal doesn't bend on its own. **It only bends when placed in the fire.**

The silence can be the fire that bends, molds, and refines you.

And THIS is the practice of Transfiguration.

Jesus. Joseph. David. Job.

Each of these moments felt like abandonment for the prophets, and yet they were moments of Divine Transformation.

The silence is never abandonment.

The silence is where the transfiguration begins.

CHAPTER 11

The Call, the Fear, and the Fallout

A Note for the Reader:

This chapter is offered in two parts. The first names what often happens after a miracle—the disorientation, collapse, and shame that can arrive once the breakthrough fades. The second moves into the lived experience of that pattern—how it feels in the body, how it plays out in real life, and how return becomes possible.

These parts are marked so you can pause if needed. Take your time here. This is important work. For when you understand this pattern, your life will work more smoothly.

Part I: Understanding the Aftershock

I know what it feels like to be called and want to step out of the calling. I understand that when this happens it can feel as though we have failed.

But I need you to hear me: You have not failed; you're just mid-journey. You're only halfway through the hike, and the top of the

The Call, the Fear, and the Fallout

mountain feels too far, but to go back to the beginning is defeating. And so you collapse. You collapse under the weight of the vision, and in that collapse the illusion of failure arises.

Here's how this moment usually unfolds:

You felt the call. You faced the fear. You took action. Then you crashed and burned.

Or maybe you gave up.

Or maybe depression or burnout hit.

Maybe you made a mistake that sabotaged your calling.

Maybe you destroyed a relationship or fell in love with the wrong person.

Maybe you fired an employee out of nowhere, or started some sort of drama in your life.

Or maybe you did your best, and you still failed . . . and paid a high price.

Or maybe . . . just maybe, you made it to the miracle and wanted to quit afterward?

If you have experienced any of these, you are not alone.

Throughout history, prophets and visionaries have been called to do the impossible: To defy logic. To step into the miraculous. To say yes to a vision far beyond their capacity.

And yet, time and time again, we see the same pattern emerge:

The Call.
The Expansion.

Transfiguration

The Resistance.
The Collapse.
and then . . .
The Return.

What we see with this pattern is that it is not enough to receive the calling. It is not enough to say yes once. We must continue to sit with God. Every day.

Without daily alignment, without the power of daily transfiguration, even the most called, the most anointed, will collapse under the weight of their own humanity.

We see it in scripture. We see it in history. And if we look closely, we see it in ourselves.

We who have been called are different. We are not like everyone else. We are driven by something beyond ourselves. We don't just receive visions—we feel them in our bones. We ache for them. We must see them come to life.

And yet, this very desire is what makes us dangerous to ourselves.

When we say yes to the call, we step into divine expansion. But if we say yes and then stop showing up—if we stop meeting with God, stop aligning ourselves, stop allowing ourselves to be transfigured—we will blow things up.

Simply because we get bored.

We were chosen to perform these miracles, to move mountains, to change the world because there is a desire inside of us that matches such a destiny.

One such morning when I was questioning my "calling" from God, these words were given to me:

The Call, the Fear, and the Fallout

—

The wild ride is the ride you chose.
You chose it because of your soul.
It is your nature. It is your wonder.
Don't shame the wild adventure you're on.
Instead, enjoy it.
This is the button you pushed.

—

This is when I began to understand this concept:

WE CHOSE this path.

Because it is our nature. Because we were indeed created for this work. Our minds and souls are hungry to spin the webs of miracles and do the impossible.

But if we run away from our callings and try to resume the "normalcy of human life," we will find that we blow things up or we avoid and quit.

You can't hold on to your old life and follow God's calling at the same time. It's like trying to drive forward while staring in the rearview mirror . . . *you're bound to crash and burn.*

Jesus said this when someone promised to follow Him wherever He went:

"No one who puts a hand to the plow and looks back is fit for the kingdom of God." Luke 9:62 (NRSV)

You can't plow a straight line if your eyes are always looking backward. The same is true in your walk with God. You must continue to look forward, move forward, and stay focused with inspired action all the time.

Transfiguration

We are wired for challenge, for the impossible, for the miraculous. And when we say yes but hesitate, doubt, or backtrack, we often unconsciously create chaos.

Or, we choose to quit.

By doing either of these, we abandon the calling we were given and avoid that it was ever given to us. And this is why it feels as if we are always bumping up against resistance.

Those who are called to extraordinary missions will feel resistance. The resistance appears when we stop taking action on the inspiration God has given us. Most of the time this isn't a conscious decision.

Oftentimes our own subconscious sabotages us because stepping into our highest potential is terrifying. It breaks all the patterns that have been running our cells from the beginning of time.

OF COURSE there is resistance.

But remember . . . YOU ARE DIFFERENT than most.

You don't thrive in normalcy. You are wired for the miraculous. You NEED the impossible.

Don't deprive yourself of the miracles that are rightly yours. You were designed to create miracles. You were created to do BIG things.

Don't run away.

Instead, transfigure to meet the greatness that God has invoked upon you.

For when we say yes to the calling and then avoid it, our bodies break down. Our businesses collapse. Our relationships suffer. We create problems just to have something to fight.

The Call, the Fear, and the Fallout

Why do those who have been called blow up their own lives? Why do we sabotage ourselves right before the breakthrough?

Because we are wired to seek expansion. And if we do not keep meeting with God, if we do not stay in daily transfiguration, *we will seek expansion elsewhere.*

We will manufacture our own chaos. We will burn our lives down just to feel the fire.

This is the great paradox of those who are called.

We love the impossible. We thrive in challenges. But if we say yes and then quit . . . we implode.

Prophets, leaders, visionaries: thrive on challenge. We need the impossible. We love proving that miracles are real, that God is real.

And yet, what happens when we say yes . . . and then hesitate? What happens when we get scared or hold back?

We get sick. We burn out. We wreck relationships. We create financial disasters. We find something to destroy because we are wired for challenge, and if we don't have one in front of us, we will manufacture one.

But what if the collapse was never meant to happen? What if we could learn from those who have gone before us? What if we could see the pattern and choose differently?

Because, there is another way.

A way to walk in divine power without being consumed by it. A way to say yes without fear of self-sabotage. A way to keep moving forward without destruction.

Transfiguration

But before we uncover the way forward, we must recognize the pattern that's kept us stuck.

This is not a new pattern. It is just the aftershock of the miracle.

Right after the breakthrough is when many of us break. The miracle was so great our system couldn't hold it—yet. We thought we'd feel invincible, complete, untouchable. But instead, we meet ordinary life: the dishes still need doing, work still calls, children still need raising.

The clash of energies is a lot for the system. Most of all, the miracle broke us open to a new version of ourselves, and the expansion outpaced our capacity.

In that aftershock, the urge shows up in two paths: quit or blow it up.

Quitting looks like running, numbing, going passive, trying to return to old patterns, or avoiding.

Blowing it up looks like picking a fight, breaking what was working, reaching for control, manufacturing chaos—anything to feel the fire we felt in the expanse, once again.

This isn't proof you're unworthy; it's proof that God is still molding you. And the vision that God has given requires you to become NEW to fully expand INTO it.

Your system needs a return to God to increase capacity. Daily transfiguration doesn't just keep you "spiritual"; it trains your nervous system and body to carry the enormity of the visions you have received.

Because there is no mountain top to camp on, you must keep going AFTER the miracle. When the miracle comes, it is essential that your system learns how to hold it.

The Call, the Fear, and the Fallout

So if you have been called, seen visions, taken action, and even witnessed miracles, only to find yourself deep in a hole afterward, you are not alone.

Part II: Living inside the Aftershock

My Aftershock

I remember when God had called me to create a TV show and to launch it at my first live event. From the stage, in five minutes, I was blessed to sell $1.25 million. A miracle beyond miracles. The show was happening!!!

Three days later, I found myself on a date with a man who was not the caliber I should have been dating. I slipped back into old ways and old energy because the new me—the TV-show host, the woman who could bring in $1.25 million in five minutes—felt so unfamiliar, so big, I didn't know how to stay **as her.** *This new me felt too big to hold.*

I didn't know how to BE that version yet. And so I fell back into old patterns that ultimately sabotaged me for months to come. I dated this man for six weeks, which led to days of intermingling my energy with someone who was not a match to my frequency and the vision God had called me to.

And then the fallout occurred . . . as I was sitting at my doctor's office with a positive STI test.

Shame destroyed me.

I began to drown in doubt, fear, and guilt.

"How could I have done this? How could I have slept with a man who had STI's???"

And then I saw it.

Transfiguration

I saw that the miracle had been too much for my system, which led me to blow my life up. The loneliness had broken me.

The loneliness of being a single mom, a CEO—and truly the loneliness of being a prophetess—had been the precursor to this moment.

But it was the struggle of not being able to be the woman who called miracles down from the heavens.

And so, I had chosen a companionship that was not aligned with who I am called to be. And the result? *Three sexually transmitted infections and three bottles of antibiotics to go with them.*

A few days later, while in the Texas airport, as I sat ready to board the plane to Miami, my phone alarm chimed to remind me to take my antibiotics.

A man beside me was visibly high on drugs; across from me, a woman dressed like a hooker stared at me. I didn't even know I was judging them until I twisted open the cap to my chlamydia medication, and I heard God say:

—

Stop looking down at the lepers from the wall, telling them you're praying for them.
It is time for you to be a leper.
Sit with them and love them.
For you are one as they are.

—

That moment broke me. And it freed me. It saved me.

And I saw two very strong truths come from this experience:

The greatness that God had called me to be was not fully able to LIVE inside of me. Not right away. And so I had blown my life up for a minute in the whiplash of the miracle.

But also . . . even mistakes I made, God used to teach me, to refine me, and ultimately to MAKE me.

These moments humbled me into a new practice.

I began meeting with God three times a day—morning, midday, and night—so my soul and my nervous system could learn to carry the visions and miracles God was giving me.

The answer wasn't to run or blow it up; the answer was return.

Sit with God. Align. Be transfigured again and again and again.

And I am not the only one who has walked this pattern.

The Proof is in the Stories

Elijah — Fire from Heaven, Fear in the Wilderness

1 Kings 18–19

The Call:
God sends Elijah to stand before Ahab and an entire nation that has drifted into idolatry. He is to rebuild the ruined altar, call the people back, and stake everything on the living God answering by fire.

The Expansion:
Elijah rebuilds the altar with twelve stones, lays the wood and the bull, digs a trench around it, and has water poured over everything three times—so much that it runs down and fills the trench. Then he prays a single, simple prayer—and the fire of the Lord falls, consuming the offering, the wood, even the stones, and licking up the water.

Transfiguration

Elijah calls fire from the heavens, a miracle beyond miracles.

The Resistance:
Even after this miracle, he is immediately hit with resistance. Jezebel vows to kill him, and terror pierces the wonder of the miracle he has received. He runs into the wilderness and collapses beneath a broom tree—exhausted, afraid, and utterly alone.

The Collapse:
There he prays to die—**"I have had enough, LORD," he said. "Take my life; I am no better than my ancestors"** (1 Kings 19:4, NIV). He had seen miracles. He had become the man who could call them forth. But immediately his life is at stake and he finds himself tired and wanting to quit. This path has become too heavy for him to carry.

The Return:
Even though he wants to quit . . . God does not leave him alone. As he sleeps, **an angel** touches him and says, "Get up and eat." Elijah looks, and there by his head is bread baked on hot stones and a jar of water. He eats and lies down again. The angel of the Lord comes a second time, touches him, and says, "Get up and eat, for the journey is too much for you." Strengthened by that food, he travels forty days and nights to Horeb.

Jonah — Swallowed by Resistance

Jonah 1–4

The Call:
"Arise, go to Nineveh."

A clear word. A hard assignment. Jonah is asked to walk into a violent city and speak what God says. God needs him to speak the truth.

The Call, the Fear, and the Fallout

The Resistance:
Jonah runs the other way—down to Joppa, ticket in hand for Tarshish, as if distance can help him avoid his calling . . . as IF he can avoid God.

A storm arises and the lots fall to Jonah. He owns it: *I'm running.* "Throw me in and the sea will quiet."

The Collapse:
He is hurled into the ocean and is swallowed deep into a whale—three days and nights in the belly of this great fish. Here he experiences pure darkness. Stripped down to prayer, he stops fighting and surrenders.

Return:
Mercy arrives. The fish releases him onto shore. The word of the Lord comes **again**—with the same assignment, same calling—but now, he is a different man. For this time, Jonah listens and does.

The Expansion:
Jonah follows his calling and in return, the city is saved. Hearts are softened and turned to God.

Moses — The Rock and the Rage

Numbers 20:1–12

The Call:
Before the assembly, God gives Moses a clear instruction: **speak** to the rock and water will flow. The moment is meant to display God's holiness, not Moses' force.

The Expansion:
His leadership has been forged inside a river of wonders: Nile waters that run red, plagues that shake Egypt, a pillar of cloud and fire that leads by day and night. The sea stands up in walls and the children of

Transfiguration

Israel walk through on dry ground; manna appears daily on the desert floor, and quail rains down in the evenings. Step after step, the rhythm is the same—trust, speak, and watch God provide.

The Resistance:
Moses's anger at the people boils over, and he rebukes the congregation as if the power were his to wield. In frustration, he lifts the staff and strikes—twice.

The Collapse:
Water gushes, but at a cost: "You did not trust Me enough to honor Me as holy before the people." Entry into the land will belong to another.

Return:
Even with consequence, God does not abandon His servant. Moses continues to lead, lays hands on Joshua, and ascends the mountain to see the promise with his own eyes.

David — When Kings Forget Their Source

2 Samuel 11–12 (with background in 1 Sam 16; 2 Sam 5–7)

The Call:
David is anointed king and a holy leader of Israel. David's life is a covenant of presence and justice. He loves God and always leads with courage and deep faith.

The Expansion:
Kingdoms fall back as David advances. He takes Jerusalem, brings the ark home with dancing and shouts, pitches a tent of praise, writes songs that heal a nation's heart. He saves many lives and runs the kingdom in peace.

The Call, the Fear, and the Fallout

The Resistance:
Peace abides and David stays home. Idleness bends desire inward; he sees Bathsheba as she bathes and sends for her, and begins to layer deception over desire.

The Collapse:
To hide his sin, he arranges for the death of Bathsheba's husband, Uriah, and sets in motion a sorrow that tears through his house. The anointed king has forgotten his calling and his God.

Return:
Nathan's parable cuts through the fog. David repents with a broken and contrite heart and accepts the consequence, and keeps walking with God—mercy restoring fellowship even as discipline remains.

Peter — Walking on Water, Sinking in Fear

Matthew 14:22–33

The Call:
"Come." One word from Jesus invites Peter into the impossible. He steps out of the boat toward the voice he trusts.

The Expansion:
At one word—"Come"—he swings his legs over the side of the boat. Wind slaps his face, spray salts his lips; still, he steps. Heel, then toe, find the impossible holding. Eyes locked on Jesus, Peter walks—water firm beneath him while the others watch, stunned, from the boat.

The Resistance:
Wind and waves surge into his awareness, and fear pries his eyes away from Christ. The outer storm becomes an inner one.

Transfiguration

The Collapse:
Faith falters and he begins to sink—proof that the miraculous cannot be carried by willpower alone.

Return:
Immediately, Jesus reaches, catches, and lifts Peter. Back in the boat, the wind dies, worship rises, and Peter learns the lesson: return your eyes, return your footing.

Elijah — Fire from Heaven, Fear in the Wilderness (1 Kings 18–19)

God sends Elijah to stand before Ahab and an entire nation that has drifted into idolatry. He rebuilds the ruined altar, calls the people back, and stakes everything on the living God, answering by fire. The fire of the Lord falls, consuming the offering, the wood, even the stones, and licking up the water. A miracle beyond miracles.

And yet, resistance follows immediately. Jezebel vows to kill him, terror pierces the wonder, and Elijah runs into the wilderness. He collapses beneath a broom tree, exhausted and afraid, and prays to die. Even then, God does not leave him. An angel feeds him—twice—and strengthens him for the journey that is still too much to carry alone.

Pattern seen.

Pattern proven.

The Called are not spared resistance; they are trained by it. And this pattern is not only ancient; it is alive now. It is alive in me. It is alive in you.

I, too, have fallen.

I, too, have been broken open by my own mistakes.

The Call, the Fear, and the Fallout

I, too, have been stripped of perfection—undone by my own humanness.

And in the dust of that breaking, I found that God always loves me. Even when I avoid my callings, or slip back into old patterns, or make wild mistakes because I don't know how to be with God's miracles, God still meets with me. Every single day.

But I have to choose to make time for that meeting.

I no longer love from the tower of perfection. I love from the dust of shared pain, from the place of imperfection and humility.

It has been in my moments of failing—avoiding God, submitting to STI tests, and worshipping fear over faith—that I have become moldable. It leads me to wonder . . . maybe this—this descent into love, this sitting in the dust—is what it truly means to be a prophet.

God did not leave me when I fell. God loved me. God still showed up, held me, and taught me. Some of the greatest miracles in history—and in my life—have come just when it seemed everything had fallen apart.

If you're reading this and fear you've missed your calling—that you stepped out in faith and failed, or made too many mistakes to be called again—remember this: people who never fall are people who never try, never trust, never step into the unknown as God asks. Those who fulfill their vision are the ones who fall and rise again, and again, and again.

Not from pride but from the dust.

From mercy. From real love.

CHAPTER 12

The Reward of the Called

Not everyone is called in this way. This is neither good nor bad.

It's just important to realize that you, indeed, are different.

And while we have seen the cost it takes to be called, there are many rewards that must be witnessed.

If you do not see the rewards, the costs might stop you right in your tracks. And while you may feel as if you do not have what it takes to keep going, let me assure you that you not only have it, **you were created FOR this.**

If comfort has never fully satisfied you, if ease has never felt like enough, if you have carried a hunger for more that you could never quite name: that is not ambition. It is not dissatisfaction.

It is memory.

The remembrance of who you DIVINELY are.

You were born with a certain soul. You have a strength that keeps rising even after repeated collapse. You have a fire that reignites after disappointment instead of going dark. But mostly, you have a hunger that refuses a small life—not because you want more, **but because you are more.**

You listen for God.

You feel alive when the stakes are high.

You see meaning where others see tragedy. And when you try to live any other way, when you choose safety over obedience, quiet over truth, comfort over calling, **life feels monotonous.**

And monotony feels like death.

It becomes muted and dim.

Like you are only surviving instead of living.

Not everyone is built to live under this kind of pressure. Not everyone can hear God this closely. Not everyone has the fire within them that is required to keep rising even when the cost keeps increasing.

But YOU are wired for this.

You were created to do something most people would never choose, which is proof that you DO have what it takes to keep going.

And not only do you have what it takes, YOU will thrive in it. **You were MADE for this.**

The cost makes sense once you know who you are. The calling costs so much because it activates everything in you: your sensitivity, your courage, your endurance, your capacity to carry God into the world.

This is why not everyone can be called in this way. And this is why you *are*.

Transfiguration

You walk when others stop. You listen when others numb out. You carry truth when it would be easier to stay silent. And you rise again and again without becoming bitter.

You were created to be a vessel for what God needs on the earth now. Once you understand this, the cost stops feeling cruel. And instead, it becomes your fuel.

My life has not gotten easier since I said yes to God. In many ways, it has actually gotten harder. The pressure has increased. The loneliness has sharpened. The fire has intensified.

And still, my life is absolutely extraordinary.

Not because circumstances improved, but because God became real.

I walk with God. I hear God. God teaches me something, and then it is given. God tells me something will happen, and then it is done.

I have watched prayer turn into provision and obedience open doors I could not force. Words have been spoken to my heart from God that then poured outward into miracles.

And this will be the same for you.

This is the reward of the called. It's not relief from pressure, but the reward is the sacred, intimate communion with God.

This is the reward that no one can take from you. For there is no joy like the presence of God. No success can ever compare to knowing:

I am seen.
I am known.
I am heard.

By the One who made me.

When you know that God is working through you and that your obedience matters—that God's work is touching Earth because you stayed in action—you are given the energy to keep walking.

You are given the fire to keep going. You are given the strength to keep being.

It is here that the calling stops draining you and *begins to fuel you.*

But it is a choice.

You get to choose this path, *or don't.*

What I have come to realize is that I would choose this life again. I would choose pressure over numbness, fire over comfort. I would choose walking with God over a monotonous life without Him.

Because there is no greater loss than living safely and never knowing God. And there is no greater reward than knowing my life is a conduit, my obedience is activating transformation, and my *"yes"* **is shaping the world.**

This is who you are. You were created for this moment. For this calling. For this work.

And once you know that, once you recognize yourself, the cost no longer scares you. Because the reward is not *someday*. The reward is aliveness. The reward is fulfillment. The reward is to know God.

Because the reward for souls such as ours is this: we get to live in the realm of miracles.

We work hand in hand with God. We speak with God. We create with God.

Transfiguration

And while the cost may be real at times, the miracles are worth it. *Every time.*

Remember who you are.

You are a miracle worker. You are one who brings light into the dark places of this earth. You are one who awakens truth within the lives of others.

Your presence shifts humanity in profound ways.

Be the prophet or prophetess you have been called to be.

For your cells know this pattern. Your soul was prepared for this work. And you have been anointed to lead.

PART III
THE LAWS OF TRANSFIGURATION

Transfiguration

> The paths that have gotten you here . . . were the perfect path to make you who you were meant to become.
>
> The struggles you have faced strengthened you.
>
> The visions began the transfiguration process.
>
> And now we allow your visions to become fully realized.

CHAPTER 13

God Is a Magnifier & Multiplier

Once you begin to remember WHO you ARE—a prophet, a prophetess, one who has been called—**then the work really begins**. This is when you become the weaver of new tapestries.

You become the one who breathes and causes hearts to change.

But the work starts *with you* and *how you meet with God.*

Whatever you bring to God, God magnifies. Whoever you are being when you meet with God, God magnifies. When you truly understand this, your experience with God transforms.

You can still come to God broken . . . just bring your brokenness when you do. Don't hide it, and don't sit in it. Give it to God, and let God transmute it.

So often, we hold onto our pain and complain to God about our problems. We ask for miracles while clinging to our suffering. That's not how God works. You can't hold onto your burdens *and* expect God to perform miracles. You don't get both.

Transfiguration

Just as your car cannot drive on two roads going in different directions, miracles and misery cannot manifest in the same space. Miracles don't work with diluted visions. You must become clear, and then you must choose.

Whatever path you're on is the path you are choosing.

Most of the time we choose suffering because it is the only pattern we have been shown. But if this is the pattern your cells know, how do you release your suffering?

I have found that there is a call to surrender.

We're often taught to "surrender our problems over to God." But I know how scary it is to hand your problems to God. I know what it feels like to carry the weight of the world on your shoulders, to finally break down enough to ask for help, only to be met with disappointment and abandonment.

If you have felt that from other people, then trusting God with your burdens might feel just as difficult. Maybe you fear that if you give your struggles to God, He might be unable, or unwilling, to take them from you.

And so, you sit with God, clinging to your problems like they are treasured possessions that only you can truly handle. After all, who would you be without them? They've been with you longer than you can remember, woven into your identity. They are familiar. They might even feel safer than the unknown beyond them.

And yet—what if the very act of surrender is what finally allows you to be held? To receive? To create miracles? To finally remember and become who you are called to be?

We don't cling to problems because we like them. We cling to avoid the pain of letting them go.

We are like the toddler throwing a tantrum over a sucker stuck in their hair. It hurts to take it out, and we still want to eat it. So we try to remove it without losing a single hair and without ruining the sucker.

This is the paradox God invites us into: be human—*and surrender your humanness.*

I was battling with this paradox when, in prayer, God showed me a vision of placing my struggles into Him, rather than simply handing them over. That is when everything changed.

I saw that my fear wasn't only in releasing them, it was the belief that if I let go, God's hands might be in His pockets and my struggles would simply fall to the ground, leaving me abandoned, as I had been by others.

Instead, I was shown:

If I place my struggles into God, I can feel them being held. I can trust that God will care for them and transmute them into something different.

And if God takes my burdens, I am clear: clear to choose differently, clear to become someone new.

Because if you place your burdens into God and ask Him to transmute them, He will.

The Law of Magnification

Who you bring to God is magnified. God does not magnify your burdens—God magnifies you.

Transfiguration

This is why it is of the utmost importance to release all that does not serve you before you sit with God. If you sit in your pain, fear, and doubt before God, those feelings will grow, not because God is punishing you, but because God magnifies what is brought before Him.

By law, God magnifies what is currently running through you.

So place your burdens into God. Let Him receive them. Let Him transmute them.

Then choose.

Choose how you want to feel. Choose what you desire to have magnified. Choose to step into the version of yourself that aligns with the vision God has for you.

Meet God as that person. Pray as that person. Have faith as that person.

And watch as the **Law of Magnification** begins to work in your life.

The Law of Multiplication

What you offer, God multiplies.

Once you have placed your burdens into God and stepped into your higher self, you are ready to give Him something tangible . . . something He can multiply beyond your imagination.

Whoever you are being when you sit with God is magnified—and from that place, what you offer is multiplied. This is the **Law of Divine Multiplication.**

But this is not wishing. There is a clear difference between wishing and becoming.

We often expect God to grant our wishes as if a simple desire is enough for a miracle to appear. But that's not how divine multiplication works.

God doesn't just give us what we ask for; **God magnifies us and then multiplies what we bring.**

Look at Christ feeding the multitude. When the people were hungry, He could have made manna fall again, but He wanted to show the law in action.

He didn't need a lot, but He needed something.

A boy brought five loaves and two fish. It was given, *so it could be multiplied.*

After the offering was given and distributed, thousands were fed, and twelve baskets of leftovers remained.

Multiplication requires participation.

God will multiply what you give. God cannot multiply what you hoard. Hoarding looks like inspiration that has not been placed into action. God cannot multiply what has not been given.

There is an abundance that is activated with God's multiplication: **when you give, there is more than enough.**

There will be overflow.

Here is what God has taught me:

Submission clears attachment to suffering.
Faith becomes the energy God magnifies.
Inspired action becomes the offering God multiplies.

Transfiguration

We can't ask God to multiply our dreams and then offer Him nothing. Our actions are the loaves and fish. Whatever we bring forward, no matter how small, God can multiply.

So ask yourself: what am I currently doing? What am I bringing to God?

Are you sitting in the crowd, belly aching with hunger, waiting, hoping that food will come? Or are you the one searching for even a single loaf to bring to God, trusting that if you offer it, He will multiply it?

If your actions don't match your desired outcome, ask: *where am I holding back in fear?*

Do I fear that if I give, it won't be returned? That if I surrender, God won't show up? That my actions won't be enough?

What has God asked me to do that I'm still gripping?

The book.
The business.
The creation I know I'm here to bring.

Am I hoarding by holding divine inspiration captive?

Do I keep putting off the calling for a day that never arrives? Or am I willing to take action—imperfect—and lay it down in front of God and ask for it to be magnified and for my offerings to be multiplied?

The invitation is this: meet God as you desire to be. This unlocks the **Law of Magnification.**

Then take action. This activates the **Law of Multiplication.**

Even if your offering is small, God multiplies.

The Practice

Place your suffering into God. Name the burden; put it INTO God. Choose who you're being. Choose how you DESIRE to feel.

Then, and only then, sit at the foot of God and ask for THIS desire to be magnified.

Then bring a "loaf of bread." Offer one small, tangible action connected to your calling.

From there, begin to watch the laws move.

God will magnify you. God will multiply what you offer.

As you have been called, it is essential that you understand these laws.

You have mighty work to do.

And when you walk in the **Laws of Magnification and Multiplication,** you will remember what you have always known deep down:

With God, all things are possible.
With God, all visions can become real.
And with God, we BECOME our greatest selves.

CHAPTER 14

The Currancy of Miracles

Miracles are not anomalies. They are a law, a frequency, a current that flows through all creation, waiting for someone awake enough to touch it.

Most people believe miracles are rare because they have forgotten how to access them. They do not understand that the same power that parts seas, multiplies loaves, and rewrites destinies is still alive and still governed by divine laws as exact as electricity or gravity.

Miracles are not granted at random. They respond to frequency. They respond to alignment. They respond to those who know how to tune their inner current to the energy of God. This is the Currancy of Miracles: the force, the flow, and the exchange through which Heaven and Earth meet.

I believe in miracles.

Actually, no—I don't just believe in them. I know them.

I know them the way I know the sun will rise. I know them the way I know breath will fill my lungs. *I know them because I live inside their rhythm.*

The Currancy of Miracles

And still, it is easy to fall for the illusion that miracles were only for ancient times: that they belonged to prophets, scribes, apostles, saints, and holy ones; that they are stories from a distant past, not living power for the present moment. If that is your truth, that is what you will see.

But there is a law that governs miracles, and a frequency that activates them. There is a way to call them forth. When you begin to understand the energetics of transfiguration, you will come to see as I see.

Miracles are not rare.

Miracles are not random.

Miracles are not gone. **Miracles are alive.**

They are not just stories in holy books, and they are not prizes given to the lucky. They are the birthright of every soul who walks with God. Miracles can be claimed, and miracles respond to the one who knows the law of their becoming. The Law of Transfiguration is the frequency that calls them forth.

Miracles are the frequency of transfiguration. When you understand this law, you can weave miracles anytime you desire. You become a conduit for God, turning impossibilities into reality, bending time, and stepping into limitless creation.

I didn't learn this because life was easy.

I was taught this law because my life was hard. In the moments of crushing pressure, I prayed, sought, asked, and surrendered. And in that surrender, God taught me the Currancy of Miracles.

The principle is simple—so simple the mind wants to reject it.

God taught me using a form I understood: electricity.

Transfiguration

Electricity runs your life without you begging it to. You flip a switch, and light appears. You do not pray for the current. You do not question whether it will work. You expect it. Miracles operate the same way. They are already present, already flowing, already sustaining. We have simply forgotten how to access them.

God revealed two words to me:

Current—the force of water or electricity

Currency—a system of value or exchange

When they meet, they form an entirely new meaning: **Currancy—the force, flow, and exchange of miracles.**

Miracles are not luck.

They are not accidents. They operate under a law just like electricity, wind, and water. When we allow ourselves to be transfigured to match God's frequency, we become the miracle workers we were destined to be.

Thomas Edison didn't create electricity—he learned to channel it into light. And this is what prophets and prophetesses do: they learn to channel an invisible force into tangible reality.

You don't need to strive for miracles. You don't need to beg for them.

You don't need to "deserve" them. Miracles are as present as oxygen—but while oxygen keeps you alive, miracles keep you awake.

You can live your entire life without accessing them. This is why so many live in the dark. We don't choose darkness because we want it; we choose it because no one taught us where the light switch is.

The truth is simple: miracles are already running.

You must step into the river. And the first step is to shift from hoping for miracles to claiming miracles.

When you claim miracles, you become a magnet for them.

Miracles don't just move around you; they move through you. If Edison learned to harness external current, God teaches us to notice the internal one.

When the current within you aligns with the **Law of Transfiguration,** you stop hoping for power and begin carrying it. Imagine a current of electricity running through your body—from your crown, down your spine, through your nervous system.

This current is real. It is measurable. It is the energy that animates your being.

This inner current is the magnet for miracles, but it only magnetizes what you are already carrying. If fear is running through your current, fear multiplies. If doubt is running through your current, doubt multiplies. If lack is running through your current, lack multiplies. The inner magnet returns what it is tuned to.

To activate the Currancy of Miracles, you must tune your current to match the frequency of miracles. As you practice the transfiguration process, you will see how simple this becomes.

And if your mind resists—good.

Doubt is always the first barrier to claiming miracles. If you find yourself thinking, "This sounds too simple," then you are fighting to keep life hard.

Resistance is the argument for limitation. It is familiar, but familiarity is not truth.

Transfiguration

One of the greatest blocks to miracles is the belief that life must be difficult. Miracles are trying to pour through you like a river. You must stop defending your limitations long enough to feel the flow.

Miracles did not die. They were simply forgotten. The same power that parted the Red Sea, raised Lazarus, opened blind eyes, and healed the paralyzed was never taken from the earth. Humans stopped believing in it.

And belief is the conductor of miracles.

Just as a house without wiring cannot produce light, a heart without belief cannot conduct miracles. Belief is the wiring. Faith is the current. Transfiguration is the frequency.

Without belief, miracles remain unseen—even if they are standing right in front of you.

We were meant to bring miracles back to this earth. You. Me. All of us.

It is time for the miracle workers to rise. You are the one who will restore faith in the impossible. You are the one who will bring light into the world.

Miracles do not simply happen around you—**they happen because of you.**

This is the Currancy of Miracles.

CHAPTER 15

Trust, Doubt, and the Language of Faith

—

May you rest in the hope.
May you find surety in the trust.
May you rejoice in the beauty.
How dare you ever doubt?
You have seen the Red Sea part.
You have watched miracles rain down from the heavens.
Do not doubt, for that is what is holding my promises from you.
Doubt is not your god.
Stop worshiping it.

—

One morning I woke up with such heavy doubt that it felt as though it had hardened inside of my chest like a brick and narrowed my vision to see only through the lens of fear. God had just called me to my next great vision, and I was tired. I felt exhausted from the last visions God had given me. But still I came to my prayer corner to sit at the foot of God and to ask.

Transfiguration

And these were the words that were given to me. Not a push forward in belief . . . but an invitation to trust deeper. Instead, God showed me that I was worshiping the god of doubt.

What we focus on, give energy to, and listen to is what we worship. And God helped me see that even though I was sitting in prayer, I wasn't worshipping God. No, I was worshipping the god of doubt.

As I sat in prayer, I was shown something I had never seen before regarding fear and doubt. Fear and doubt are not personal flaws. They are not sins. They are not signs that you are failing. They are a language.

So are faith and trust. But they are an entirely different dialect.

We only speak the languages we've been taught. If I asked you if you speak Russian or Japanese, most of you would say no. And you wouldn't shame yourself for that. You would simply understand that you were never taught these languages, and so therefore you do not speak them.

We speak the languages of our families, the languages of our cultures, the languages of the environments that shaped us. And for many of us, fear and doubt were the first languages we learned. They were how we learned to survive, how we learned to stay alert. We were raised in homes, communities, even religions where fear and doubt were the primary dialects. It was how we learned to relate to the world.

So when doubt or fear appears, it does not mean something has gone wrong. It means an old dialect has reasserted itself.

And the good news about language is this: *you can learn a new one.*

But this law matters more for those who have been called, because fear and doubt plague us more than they do the average person. The greater your light, the greater the resistance. And so you feel the intensity of fear and doubt in ways most will never experience. Yet, when you understand the Law of Language, you will no longer be held hostage.

Fear and doubt are the voices of darkness.

They whisper. They creep. They mimic the voices of people we love. And because they often speak in the tone of our ancestors or our upbringing, we mistake them for part of us. We believe they are family.

But while fear and doubt may be familiar, they are not aligned with our higher calling. If we do not replace these languages with a new language, they will destroy our energy, hijack our happiness, and dismantle the very callings God has placed upon us.

And this is where the trap lives.

A miracle proves God is real—but it does not automatically teach the body how to trust Him. This is why doubt and fear so often shows up after miracles, not before them. You think that once God has proven Himself, fear should disappear. But the nervous system has not learned the new language yet.

The miracle happened, but the system is still speaking fear. And when the language doesn't change, confusion returns, even in the presence of proof.

This is where people burn out. This is where they start controlling outcomes God never asked them to manage. This is where they exhaust themselves trying to carry something that was meant to move through them, not be held by them. Not because they are weak, but because fear is driving the system.

The **Law of Language** is a law of transfiguration.

Transfiguration

This law is easy to miss because fear and doubt are so familiar to our systems that we don't even realize they are running. But the power of a prophet is this: when they see, they cannot unsee.

When you begin to notice your relationship to fear and doubt, you will no longer be able to unsee how they have been governing your life. And when you understand that fear and doubt are simply a dialect you were taught—and that the language of God is faith and belief—your relationship to fear and doubt begins to change.

So how do you learn to speak the language of God fluently?

The same way you would learn any language.

You immerse yourself. You spend more time with God. You ask God to teach you this language. And you surround yourself with others who also speak it.

Fear is more contagious than any illness in the world. But faith is just as contagious.

Place yourself among those who speak the language of God. And when you notice yourself slipping back into speaking fear, worshiping fear, dragging doubt along for the journey—pause.

Sit with God, even if it is only in your heart. Ask for a translation. Ask God to translate fear into faith, doubt into trust. Ask Him to alchemize your energy so it matches the frequency of miracles.

This is how you enact the law of transfiguration at any place, day, or time. You transfigure when you translate your language to match God's.

And when you ask for that translation, you are not just asking to feel different. You are asking to learn.

Trust, Doubt, and the Language of Faith

You learn the language of God by sitting with Him. By listening. By turning your ears to match the frequency of God's voice.

But language is not mastered through listening alone. Fluency comes through use. And this is where co-creation begins.

God is a master builder. A master builder needs building materials just as a master writer needs words. God magnifies and builds using the raw materials we give Him. And the raw materials we give Him are our words and thoughts.

This is where the language of faith is actually practiced.

The only way to become fluent in the languages of trust and faith is to co-create with God. When you co-create with God, you begin to understand His energy, His timing, His blueprints.

Faith does not grow in theory. It grows in partnership.

God does not build with confusion. God is not the author of murkiness. Clarity is the energy of God. When your inner language is unclear, what you build will be unstable. When your inner language is clear, faith becomes usable.

Give God clear instructions.

The precision of your ask is the magnet for the result you are seeking.

And then take action.

Trust is built through action.

When you take inspired action, fear and doubt lose their footing. They cannot survive inside co-creation with God.

Transfiguration

I've watched this happen in my own life. When I pray from fear, my prayers are vague. When I pray from doubt, my vision scatters. But when I stop, notice the language I'm speaking, and consciously return to God, clarity returns.

My asks sharpen.

My next step becomes obvious. My body settles. Nothing outside of me changes at first, but everything inside of me does.

And from that place, movement becomes possible again.

So when fear or doubt rise, don't fight them.

Don't shame them. Notice the language. Place it into God. Ask for a translation. Ask for faith and trust to be activated within you. Ask for your inner language to align with God's frequency.

Then take one clear, inspired action.

This is how faith is built. This is how miracles move.

—

Like the web of a spider, no two journeys are the same.
How dare you doubt?
I have led you here.
Stay in faith.
The path has already been paved.
The story has already been written.
Trust my hand.
I will guide you.
The arrival will be sweet.

—

Faith and trust are the languages of God.

They are available to you. You are not owned by fear and doubt. . . . They are just a language.

And now you are simply learning how to speak differently.

Sit with God.

Ask for translation.

Ask—and then receive.

CHAPTER 16

The Edge

To push the edge is to flirt with death.
Not a physical death—but a soul-quaking death. A death of identity, a death of illusion, a death of the self that's too small to carry the bigness of your becoming.

Pushing to the edge means pushing until you feel like you might die.

It means stepping into something so unknown, so stretching, so holy, that your body panics and your mind tries to run. You lie in bed, your body tensing, your mind racing, your breath shaking, and you say to yourself, *"I might actually die because of this calling."*

This is not an accident.

This is the **Law of the Edge** at work. This is what happens when you follow the visions God gives you.

Your visions will scare you. They will stretch you. They will ask for more than you think you can give. They will lead you to a place you've never been before—to the edge of what's familiar, the edge of your conditioning, the edge of your strength.

And this is where most people turn back. They retreat and collapse, or they run toward comfort, safety, and what they've always known.

Not because they're weak, but because the edge feels like death. And in a way, *it is*.

This moment collapses you. This moment destroys you. This moment sends you retreating into the only place that feels familiar—the past. A past built from wounds, a past built from trauma, a past identity created just to survive.

But to cross the threshold into transformation, *you have to sit in this space.*

This moment shows up after many different actions—maybe after a bold decision, a deep declaration, or a vulnerable act of expression. It arrives when you commit to God and the visions God has for you.

The moment is intense.

This is where your nervous system fires and fear hijacks your thoughts. You feel unsafe, unloved, and rejected. You might want to run away and pretend it never happened. You might want to collapse into shame and grief.

This is what happens when we ask to be transfigured.

And if you are here now, reading this, then know you are not losing your mind. You are not failing. You are standing inside the **Law of the Edge.**

In these moments the soul is saying, *"God, use me. Burn away what no longer serves."* But then, when fire comes, our soul takes a back seat and our mind begins to freak out. We might feel like we're dying. We might want to give up. We might think we want to die.

Transfiguration

But this is the fire of transfiguration—the fire of becoming, the fire that refines.

This is what Moses felt when Satan came to deceive him. Satan tempted him and told him that he was nothing, and Moses almost believed him. But then Moses spoke out loud:

"Now, for this cause I know that man is nothing, which thing I never had supposed.
I am a son of God, in the similitude of His Only Begotten."
Moses 1:12-13 (The Pearl of Great Price)

Moses remembered what it felt like to be with God, and in that remembrance he reclaimed his power. Moses understood the **Law of the Edge.** He saw that this moment was not about survival but surrender.

He did not argue with the fire. He did not negotiate with the fear. He offered the self that could not survive this calling, and in return God restored him in truth.

Right now, darkness wants to shape you. It wants to tell you stories. It wants to loop fear throughout you. It wants to convince you that you are unworthy.

Because if you collapse here, if you give up now, then the version of you who carried the dream, the vision, the calling—that version dies. *And darkness wins.*

But if you understand what's really happening, **you win.**

If you stay, if you hold steady in the fire, if you remember who you are, you won't die.

Actually . . . wait.

The Edge

That's not quite true.

Something does die.

The you that worships *fear dies*. The you that believes *false illusions dies*. The you that *latches to monotony for safety dies*.

This is the offering the **Law of the Edge** requires—not your life but the version of you that cannot go where God is taking you.

You offer the old self into the fire, and in return newness is given. But the exchange only happens through death.

This is the cost of the edge, and it is also its purpose.

Because the **Law of the Edge** is ruthless in one way and merciful in another: it only takes what cannot go with you.

And when you sit in the intensity of these deaths, when you let this fire burn what needs to burn, when you see it for what it is—the reclamation of your divine inheritance—then the death is holy.

And then you rise.

You rise from the ashes, you rise in power, you rise in truth.

And this is what transfiguration really looks like.

Every time you come this close to the edge, the same law is enacted: transformation is activated at the point where the old self can no longer survive.

When the burning ends, something truer remains.

Now comes the holy work—*the work of loving what's left.*

CHAPTER 17

Where Power Meets the Wound

Every initiation has a second threshold.
The first threshold is the fire—the calling, the vision, the edge where you are asked to become more than you have ever been. But the second threshold is quieter and far more intimate. It is the moment after the fire when the mission has led you straight into the places you learned to survive.

This is not a detour. It is actually by design.

God does not give visions that avoid your wounds. God gives visions that bring you back to them—so they can finally be transfigured. The edge strips away what cannot come with you, and what remains is not polished or complete. It is tender. It is unfinished. It is human.

Loving what's left is the final initiation. It is how the prophet integrates power without fracture and how the mission becomes a place of healing instead of harm.

After the fire strips away everything you thought you were, you sit in the stillness. The shaking stops. The fear quiets. And all that's left is you. Not the you who performs. Not the you who pretends.

Not the you who hustles to be worthy. Just . . . you.

And this is the moment.

This is the sacred "T" in the road where many run away—because what rises after the fire is not polished.

It's raw. It's honest. It's loud and messy and emotional.

But this is also the place where real love begins. Because once the fire has burned away what doesn't belong, you're finally ready to see what does.

This part awakens when we get close to the edges,—the edges that bring us to the fire with God. They show up because God asks us to BECOME. And in the becoming, we must do what no longer feels safe.

BECOMING is where we freak out because it challenges our patterns—not just mental patterns but the patterns stored in our cells. This is where most people collapse because the growth that comes to those who say yes to God's calling awakens past trauma.

The visions and callings God gives us often mimic our past trauma. This isn't because God is mean, but because God is healing us through them.

God has given me visions and callings that required me to do things that made me feel alone, unsafe, and like the sacred inside of me was being unveiled without protection. This mirrored the trauma I experienced as a child when I was sexually abused. Back then I felt alone. I felt unsafe. I felt the sacred unveiled without protection.

Transfiguration

But this time—with the visions and callings God gave me, and by walking through them with God—God helped me re-wire that trauma through my callings.

As I took inspired actions toward the visions God anointed me with, God held me. He held me when I felt alone. He helped me create safety within myself as I charged toward goals that felt physically impossible. I did this with faith as the only ground beneath my feet, and God held me.

As I did this, God took the experiences that looked so much like my past trauma and transformed them into victories. He reframed trauma as transformation. I relived the past in a new context.

As I took steps that were led by God, breathed with the cadence of God, and asked for my cells to match the visions God was giving me, my trauma was rewired. And as I allowed God to rewire me, I saw the results—results that inspired and moved other humans to take action on their visions and callings.

I watched God fulfill the anointing for my life—the miracle of helping others hear His voice and speak His words. I watched my actions activate hundreds of leaders to heal the world with their own sacred books. I saw this because I stayed with the visions, even when they felt like trauma at first.

I sat at the foot of God even when the enormity of these impossible callings summoned the deepest pain of my past. Each day I asked Christ to touch my cells so they matched the cellular patterns of the visions and callings God was giving me. I was blessed to witness miracles equal to the Red Sea parting and manna falling from the heavens.

And I believe this is the pattern of the prophets.

Loving What's Left — Healing at the Edge

God's callings for you will most likely mirror your past wounds. And when you see your vision, its fire will bring you full healing and completion.

As I was channeling this chapter, God showed me something I had never seen before: the very calling placed on Moses's life mirrored his original trauma. This wasn't an accident. This was by sacred design.

Moses was born into danger. Pharaoh had commanded that all Hebrew baby boys be killed. To save him, his mother placed him in a woven basket and sent him floating down the Nile. He was abandoned, not from lack of love but because of it. And yet, to his infant body and nervous system, it was still abandonment.

That trauma imprinted.

He was raised in Pharaoh's house, close to power but disconnected from his people. He didn't fully belong to either world.

And then, years later, God gave Moses a vision.

"Go back."

Go back to the palace. Go back to the people who discarded you. Go back to the place where your identity was split. Go back to the scene of your original trauma. But this time—don't just visit. Lead.

God didn't just give Moses a mission. God gave him a mirror. And it terrified him. Of course it did. The call reactivated the very place of pain that had never been healed.

Moses wasn't just afraid of Pharaoh. He was afraid of being abandoned again.

But here's what you need to see: the calling was the healing. God asked Moses to walk into the very space that once wounded him so

Transfiguration

that this time he could walk in as the anointed one and be healed himself.

This is what God does. He doesn't give random visions. He gives visions that revisit the wound—not to traumatize us but to transfigure us.

The place that once rejected you is the place you are now called to lead from. The story that once broke you is the story God will use to set others free. And the very place where you once felt powerless is now the place where your power begins.

Because this time, you don't collapse. This time, you rise.

So when the vision terrifies you, when the calling feels like a replay of your most vulnerable memories, don't run.

Stay.

Walk with God into the fire.

PART IV
THE PRACTICE

Transfiguration

Each morning we rise from our beds to meet the day ahead.

Sleep allows us to be rested and prepared for the efforts of the new day. There is a preparation needed to accomplish the work before us.

Similarly, may we prepare ourselves to meet with the ONE TRUE God.

May we lay our minds down before God like Moses laid down his shoes before he met with God.

May we ask that our burdens and fears be cleansed from our lips like Isaiah did with the burning coal from the altar.

This is the preparation that will lead you to not just sit with God but to walk in stride with the frequency of miracles.

CHAPTER 18

May We Prepare to Sit at the Foot of God

How many times have you sought Divine connection, longing to hear God's voice, yet feeling distant . . . like something was missing?
I spent years in that space: reading my scriptures, praying, seeking God in every way I knew how.

Nine years ago, I was in a season of deep seeking. I wanted to hear God. Not just in the rules and commandments; I wanted a personal experience with God.
I WANTED TO KNOW GOD.

I craved clarity, so I turned to the scriptures and asked God to speak directly to me through the words on the page. Every morning, I would randomly flip open scriptures, trusting that whatever passage appeared was meant for me.

Then, the impossible happened. For five days in a row, I landed on the exact same scripture. *Five days in a row.* With thousands of pages in

Transfiguration

the scriptures, it was impossible for me to land on the same verses *five days in a row*.

But God was trying to teach me a principle that would change my life forever.

"I saw also the Lord sitting upon a throne, high and lifted up, and his train filled the temple.
Above it stood the seraphim; each one had six wings; with twain he covered his face, and with twain he covered his feet, and with twain he did fly.
And one cried unto another, and said: Holy, holy, holy, is the Lord of Hosts; the whole earth is full of his glory.
And the posts of the door moved at the voice of him that cried, and the house was filled with smoke.
Then said I: Wo is unto me! for I am undone; because I am a man of unclean lips; and I dwell in the midst of a people of unclean lips; for mine eyes have seen the King, the Lord of Hosts.
Then flew one of the seraphim unto me, having a live coal in his hand, which he had taken with the tongs from off the altar;
And he laid it upon my mouth and said: Lo, this has touched thy lips; and thine iniquity is taken away, and thy sin purged.
Also I heard the voice of the Lord, saying: Whom shall I send, and who will go for us? Then I said: Here am I; send me.
And he said: Go and tell this people—Hear ye indeed, but they understood not; and see ye indeed, but they perceived not.
Make the heart of this people fat, and make their ears heavy, and shut their eyes—lest they see with their eyes, and hear with their ears, and understand with their heart, and be converted and be healed.
Then said I: Lord, how long? And he said: Until the cities be wasted without inhabitant, and the houses without man, and the land be utterly desolate;

And the Lord have removed men far away, for there shall be a great forsaking in the midst of the land."

2 Nephi 16:1–12, Comparable to Isaiah 6 (The Book of Mormon)

Then, I heard God speak to me:
"Cleanse yourself before you meet with Me."

It was a command and an invitation all at once.

At first, I didn't fully understand. I was already reading my scriptures. I was already praying. I was already seeking God. *But God was asking for more.*

God was teaching me that before I entered sacred space, my body must also be prepared. Just as Isaiah cleansed his lips with coal, I was to cleanse myself before meeting with God.

That was when I created a daily practice, inspired by the verses above, that I called **The Prayer of Light**. And for the past nine years, I have said this prayer before every coaching session, every podcast, every sales call, every stage I speak on, and every hard conversation I have ever had to face in life.

> **The Prayer of Light**
> *I ask . . .*
> *That light may touch my ears so that I may hear as God hears,*
> *That light may touch my third eye so that I may use all of my spiritual gifts,*
> *That light may cleanse my lips so that I may speak the words I have been called to speak.*

Transfiguration

For a long time, this prayer was enough. But that changed the year my marriage was ending. It seemed God knew I would need deeper strength, deeper inspiration, and deeper divine intervention during such a time of pain, trauma, and loneliness.

That's when God showed me *to bless water every morning, then bless my body with this water before meeting with God.*

The same way Moses had to remove his sandals before he stepped onto holy ground. The same way Isaiah had to be cleansed with coals before receiving his commission. The same way the priests of the temple had to wash before entering the Holy of Holies.

Through this inspiration, God was showing me: *Prepare with devotion and you will be met with devotion.*

This was my missing piece. I had spent years trying to connect with God through my mind. Through scriptures. Through knowledge. Through study. Through following the rules, obeying commandments. *Trying to earn my way to God.* Believing that the more perfect I was, the more religious I was in doing the checklist; then, and only then—*I would know God.*

But, what I was looking for was only found in sacred devotion. I found God in the sacred ritual of cleansing and preparing to sit with God.

I found God *AS I WAS.*

In my imperfection.
In my mistakes.
In my unholiness.

I could be all of my imperfection **and** sit with God.

But there was a preparation needed. Not PERFECTION . . . only preparation.

May We Prepare to Sit at the Foot of God

Isaiah could not receive fully until his lips were touched with the coal. Moses could not meet with God without first preparing himself on sacred ground. Similarly, I was to bless my body before I was to meet with God.

But this is not new.

Across all faiths, water is used to cleanse, bless, and consecrate—the practice of purification before meeting with God exists in every sacred tradition.

Moses & the priests (Exodus 30:18–21) — God commanded Moses to create a bronze basin for the priests to wash their hands and feet before entering the tabernacle.

Jewish Mikvah — This is a ritual immersion in water before sacred events, symbolizing purification and readiness to receive Divine presence.

Christian Baptism — A sacred cleansing before stepping into spiritual rebirth and commitment to God.

Islamic Wudu (Ablution) — Before prayer, Muslims wash their face, hands, and feet, preparing their bodies and souls to meet with Allah.

Hindu Sacred Bathing — Pilgrims cleanse in the Ganges River before spiritual ceremonies, symbolizing the washing away of impurities.

Shinto Temizuya (Japan) — Before entering a shrine, worshippers ritually cleanse hands and mouth to prepare for communion with the Divine.

Native American Sweat Lodge — A ritual purification using steam and prayer before entering sacred rites.

Transfiguration

These examples show that water has always been used in devotion—and that we are far more alike in our worship than we think. God is not partial; God is the same God, *no matter how you worship.*

These holy practices also remind us of three things:

To *prepare* the body is to honor God.
To *wash* the body is to clear the channel for revelation.
To *annoint* the hands, the mouth, the heart—his is how we humbly and powerfully *sit at the foot of God.*

Through this inspiration, I created my own practice of preparation.

This practice has become my daily bread, the rhythm of my breath, and the ground that has held me through my most turbulent times. But . . . I want to place a disclaimer here: this is not THE way.

It is just *A way.*

The Transfiguration Blessing is a practice to try on—to begin to find *your* way. I teach you this to give you ingredients for you to sit with God and ask to build the recipe of devotion that is uniquely yours.

As I deepened my time in prayer, I felt the desire to wear a **prayer shawl**, for this was my physical sign to God that I was entering sacred communion. Each time I placed my prayer shawl on my head . . . my soul would rise. It was an outward signal that I was preparing to meet with God.

I also felt called to create a space that was dedicated to my meeting with God. And so I placed a tent on my land where I would watch the sun rise over the mountains each morning as I prayed.

It was in that tent that the blessing of the body was given to me. What moves me most is not *what* I received, but *when* I received it—not when I felt holy, not when life was working, but in the most tumultuous season of my life. *My twenty-year marriage was ending, and everything I thought I knew about my future was unraveling.*

In that season, within the army-green walls of my tent and the silence of early mornings, God taught me how to bless my body with water.

I felt inspired to buy a white clay pitcher, and I kept it filled with water. At the base of it sat a white clay bowl. Each morning I poured fresh water from the pitcher into the bowl. Then I settled onto a prayer mat I had blessed and anointed to be the place where I would sit with God.

As the sun would rise, I would lift my prayer shawl over my head . . . a shawl I had blessed with the holy water and anointed to be my sacred outward expression of devotion, a sign that I would quiet my mind and submit to God.

A submission to a higher knowing.

I would place my hands over the water and ask that Christ would *touch this water* so that it would be cleansed and purified. I asked that the water would be transformed down to its molecular structure to match the frequency of miracles.

And then I would take my right hand, dip it into this holy water, and place the water on each chakra of my body—*cleansing, clearing, and activating* all of them to match the frequency of God.

This was my practice every morning.
The tent was my place of safety.
It was my holy temple.

But when my life shifted, when my marriage officially ended, and I had to leave my sacred land that faced the mountains and the sunrise—my tent became an ancient ruin of what was once sacred and holy.

Transfiguration

And so I had to re-create the sacred in my new life. My bedroom in my own home became my sacred tent. My prayer corner no longer faced the sunrise over the mountains. Instead, it was in a house smashed in between hundreds of other houses in the middle of the city.

My prayer corner was no longer contained in a space reserved for the sacred. It was now tucked in the corner of a bedroom that held the bed where I slept and the desk I used to build my business.

Still, I dedicated space for this holy work. I built a prayer corner in the far-right edge of that room and dedicated it solely to meeting with God.

My prayer mat lay on the ground of that corner. The same white pitcher sat filled with water for a daily pouring of purification and preparation. My prayer shawl and prayer journal were always placed there in reverence for the daily meeting with God.

I learned that while I loved meeting God in my sacred tent, and praying as I looked out the tent doors at the sun peeking over the mountain range ahead . . .
The real sacredness was in the practice. No matter where I was . . . God would meet me.
The practice was not connected to a location.

The practice was in me.

Throughout the next few years, as I built my publishing house, I traveled every other week for two full years. I lived out of hotels, Airbnbs, and private islands—and this practice came with me, because it was not tied to a location . . .

It was tied to my heart.

And because of that . . . I never missed a single daily meeting with God.

May We Prepare to Sit at the Foot of God

I found myself praying in sketchy hotels in North Carolina; in the busy energy of Miami—high above the chaos, I would sit in my hotel room with water in a coffee mug that had become holy.

I found myself sitting on the top of the sacred island in the British Virgin Islands—my water in a sacred bowl I had traveled across the ocean with—overlooking the endless ocean as I watched the sun rise.

I had a beautiful prayer corner in Cabo where I would sit on a private beach with my bowl, my prayer shawl, and God.

I sat on my prayer mat in a hotel room in Saudi Arabia with my prayer shawl and met with God in the sacred—thousands of miles from home.

I had a sacred prayer corner in a gazebo in Costa Rica where I would meet with God and bless my body as I looked out at the jungle in front of me while howler monkeys in the trees above greeted the morning with me.

I have sat on the holy ground of Japan in the early mornings at the base of a Shinto shrine. And as the mist would creep up the mountain, I would sit with my prayer bowl, my prayer shawl, and my prayer journal to meet with God.

I have stayed in dingy hotels in Vegas for work . . . where I'd find a corner of the room and prepare it to meet with God.

In each place, I cleansed and prepared the space to be a prayer corner. In every hotel, in every land, I always began by asking that Christ would touch the walls, the ceilings, the floors, the trees, the beds, the chairs, the earth—whatever was in the space—and cleanse and clear it.

As Christ touched the space, I asked it to be activated to match the frequency of miracles.

Transfiguration

I asked that it be blessed and prepared for my meeting with God. And then—I would go into the sacred blessing of the body.

While my life has been wild, uncertain, scary at times, thrilling at others . . . there has been one consistent thing: *my daily prayer corner.* This practice isn't something you do only when it's easy, or only when you are at home. This practice is daily devotion.

We are to meet with God daily.

And as I deepen my devotion to God . . . I deepen in strength, in clarity, and in miracles. This is not a checklist, *this is a way of living.*

Devotion is not a *to do* . . . it is an honor.

And as you honor God, you will begin to speak and breathe miracles.

CHAPTER 19

The Sacred Centers

What began in my tent as a private ritual between God and me has become a sacred blessing I carry daily—and now share with those who walk with me. This blessing is devotion, a holy act of preparation. And while it started as something deeply personal, God made it clear: this practice was never meant to stay with me. It was given to be shared.

I remember the first time God told me to teach this blessing to a client. We were on an Author Adventure—a sacred retreat where I guide authors to channel the book they were born to write. One night, as I went to sleep, God told me to teach my client the blessing of the body. I pushed back. This felt far too sacred to share. *I questioned God.*

And then I heard:

—

This is not your practice.

—

I smiled, because of course . . . it wasn't mine. *How dare I hold it only for me?*

Transfiguration

The practice felt so personal, so woven into the very fibers of who I am. It seemed like it belonged to me and God alone. But it was never meant to be mine. It was meant to be given.

So the next morning, I sat with my client under the Sedona morning sky, the warmth of the Arizona sun pouring down over us. We were wrapped in stillness, seated before towering red rocks, and I taught her the blessing of the body. I watched it shift something in her, and I felt it shift something in me. That moment became a new beginning.

From that day forward, I have taught this practice to every author who comes to write their book with me. The practice has become the catalyst for their writing—the ignition point, the sacred activation. I have watched them continue this practice long after our author adventure has ended. I've watched this daily practice anchor them, transform them, and unite them with the sacred again and again.

I offer this blessing not as the owner of this practice but as a steward. This practice has echoes in every religion, every sacred tradition, every path of devotion. It was taught to me, but it belongs to all of us.

I also don't claim it as the right way. There is No One "Right" Way. But this is A way—a sacred way to prepare, to sit at the foot of God in reverence and receiving.

The locations on my body that I bless are the same; they are the chakras of the body. But the prayers and words I speak are different each time. I believe this blessing will become your own, that you and God will weave it together, and that your daily devotion will become a dance that is seamless between you and God. Because sacred devotion is where we meet with God.

You can do this blessing in your sacred prayer corner, or in the corner of a hotel room, or in your closet, or your backyard. You choose, because this blessing is not reserved for temples or chapels or sacred lands.

YOU are the sacred land. YOU are the holy building. YOU are the one who is being prepared.

And wherever you are, this blessing will meet you, because God will meet you in sacred devotion every time.

The Blessing of the Body

This practice is done with water—water that you bless, water that becomes holy through your words, your ASK, and your partnership with God. You then place this sacred water on each of the chakras in your body, which are energetic places that hold memory, emotion, and potential. When you cleanse these centers, you are blessing them to raise your energetic frequency.

The prayers I speak are connected to the purpose of each chakra. The sacred water and blessing compound and amplify the power of each sacred center. For those who are new to chakras, I've included a simple guide. This is devotional alignment, a returning of the body to truth. When we bless these sacred energetic centers, we raise the frequency of our body and prepare ourselves to walk in miracles.

Below is a guide to the chakras I bless daily. These are the truths I've come to know, not through reading but through practice, revelation, and experience.

Blessing of the Body Chakra Centers

Crown Chakra (top of the head)
This is the portal to God—the door you hold open or closed to divine connection. It is also where you cleanse the Center Column of your

being, the magnet for everything you are attracting into your life. Cleansing this chakra is extremely important for welcoming new revelation and inspiration.
When blessed: It becomes the gateway to revelation and spiritual clarity.

Third Eye Chakra (center of the forehead)
This is where your spiritual gifts live—your knowing, your sight, your ability to discern. This is where you claim your gifts so they partner with you in your calling.
When blessed: It activates vision, intuition, and discernment.

Eyes
You bless the eyes to see truth—to see through illusion, to see clearly, to see as God sees.
When blessed: You become a witness of truth.

Ears
You bless the ears to hear God, clearing anything that has blocked God's voice and attuning them to the frequency of God's voice so you may hear with clarity and precision.
When blessed: You receive God's messages with greater power, potency, and clarity.

Nose
This is the place of receptivity. You bless the nose to be cleared of every block that would keep you from receiving all that God has for you, so receiving becomes as effortless as breathing.
When blessed: You are prepared to receive miracles, revelation, and truth with ease.

Lips
You bless the lips to speak the words you are called to speak, cleansing and anointing them to speak with God so you can speak into existence

the worlds you are meant to build.

When blessed: Your words become instruments of alignment, power, and creation.

Throat Chakra (base of the throat)

This is your center of voice and visibility. When it's closed, it's easy to hide, silence your voice, and fear being seen. As it is cleared and activated, you become liberated and fully alive in your message, gifts, and calling.

When blessed: Your voice uncaps and is liberated; you allow others—and yourself—to see and hear you as God does.

Back of the Head (base of the skull)

Here is where looping thoughts live—the trauma patterns and subconscious programming.

When blessed: You break loops, return to truth, release mental clutter, and rest in divine knowing until the only loop that runs through you is truth.

C-7 (base of the neck, spine)

This is a center point of the nervous system where burnout and frantic energy collect.

When blessed: Overstimulation flushes out, endurance increases, and you remain in the frequency of miracles.

Front Heart Chakra (left chest)

This is where walls form from pain—fear of rejection, betrayal, and being unlovable.

When blessed: Heart walls soften and the body moves in the frequency of God, which is love.

Back Heart Chakra (left back)

This is where bitterness and resentment hide.

Transfiguration

When blessed: Mercy washes the hardness away and compassion, forgiveness, and grace unfold.

Front Solar Plexus (below the sternum)
This is the seat of procrastination and stagnation.
When blessed: It becomes divine motion—action with clarity and the stride of God.

Back Solar Plexus (mid-back)
This is where victim energy lives.
When blessed: It becomes your alchemical center, transforming fear and doubt into faith and belief.

Navel Chakra (over the belly button)
This is where attachment lives.
When blessed: You enter sacred surrender and allow God to lead every result.

Sacral Chakra (low belly)
This is where shame hides and creation is either birthed or stagnates.
When blessed: It becomes the seedbed of Divine creation and co-creation with God.

Root Chakra (base of the spine)
This is the ground wire of your being.
When blessed: Abundance activates and you live in divine supply.

Hands
Bless the hands to create as God creates.
When blessed: Your hands become God's hands.

Feet
Bless the feet to walk as God walks.
When blessed: They move in faith, make ground holy, and help you remember who you are.

Now that you've learned the sacred centers, these are the places you'll bless each day with your sacred water—crown to feet, center by center. With your body prepared, we step into the next movement: **Sacred Submission and the Washing of Mercy**, where you place into God what you're carrying, let mercy wash you clean, and ready your cells to be re-coded by Christ.

CHAPTER 20

The Sacred Submission and the Washing of Mercy

Sacred submission and sacred surrender are the next steps as we prepare to be blessed with the transfiguration blessing. Sacred submission is our willingness to give up our will, and sacred surrender is where we place our struggles into God.

One morning, I received these words from God:

—

Surrender is the locket I placed on your charm bracelet.
It's the token to the kingdom you seek.
Surrender is the holy and is the thread that weaves all miracles together.
This is the alphabet of God; it holds the tones and frequencies held within the form of God.

—

If surrender is the thread that weaves all miracles together, then this chapter is one of the most important. Sacred submission and sacred

The Sacred Submission and the Washing of Mercy

surrender is a path that many do not walk, but it is here that we find relief and support in a way that only God can provide.

Sacred Submission

In sacred submission, we have the opportunity to give up the things that pull us away from alignment. There is a difference between what our body wants and what our soul wants, and true power comes when the two are in union. The body desires, and while we may experiment, anything that is not a union between body, soul, and God is a distraction from our calling. Miracles exist in the unification of these three.

When we honor only what the body wants and go against our knowingness, it is like hearing beautiful, pure notes—played at the wrong time. The notes themselves are perfect, but their timing makes them painful to hear. What the body wants is beautiful and good, but when it is separate from our soul's knowing, it harms us and distracts us from our purpose. But when the body and soul are played together in harmony, guided by Divine inspiration, their unified energy brings us deep peace and rest.

This is what the Bible means by "casting off the natural man." We find this same concept in the Buddhist scriptures, the Yoga Sutras, the Qur'an, and dozens of other sacred texts. We don't need to deny the pleasures of our body, but those pleasures must align with our soul and our Divine discernment. When the body and soul are in unity, guided by God, we become instruments of miracles.

And each day as we prepare to meet with God, we ask that our soul, our body, and divine inspiration will be unified. We ask that we will let go of all the human vices, the cravings of the natural man, and become one with the Divine.

Transfiguration

This is much easier said than done. Human desires are often louder than divine inspiration. I remember one morning I was in the struggle of such human desires and wanted to plug my ears to the voice of God. But as I went to receive my daily blessing from God, I heard these words:

—

Today it rains.
It rains abundance, it rains inspiration, it rains freedom, it rains joy.
Today it rains because you honored My will and not yours.
Celebrate yourself and choose this life every day.

—

In my experience, the highest pleasure is found in co-creation with God. And to co-create, I get to surrender my body's cravings, my human impulses, and my earthly desires in exchange for God's will. It is here that I receive the deeper fulfillment my soul longs for. I might have to give up something that feels good in the moment, but it is always in exchange for something greater. I sacrifice not to lose but to gain the deeper, more meaningful results—results my soul already agreed upon before I even came to this earth.

This is sacred submission.

Sacred submission is an integral part of transfiguration. Through submission, we trade our plans for God's higher plans. Sacred submission activates the deepest levels of faith. We lay it all on the altar with God and trust that God will step forward and make the exchange. This is our offering for the miracle we seek.

Sacred submission reminds me of the story of Abraham and Isaac.

One day, God tested Abraham.

The Sacred Submission and the Washing of Mercy

"And he said, Take now thy son, thine only son Isaac, whom thou lovest, and get thee into the land of Moriah; and offer him there for a burnt offering upon one of the mountains which I will tell thee of."
Genesis 22:2 (KJV)

This was the son Abraham had waited for, the child God had promised would make his descendants as numerous as the stars. And yet, now God was asking for that promised son to be laid on the altar. With unwavering faith, Abraham obeyed. He rose early in the morning, saddled his donkey, and took Isaac and two servants on the three-day journey to the mountain.

When they arrived, Abraham turned to his servants: "And Abraham said unto his young men, Abide ye here with the ass; and I and the lad will go yonder and worship, and come again to you."
Genesis 22:5 (KJV)

Even in this moment, Abraham's faith was evident. He did not say *I* will come back, but instead he said *we* will return.

As they climbed the mountain, Isaac, unaware of the test, carried the wood for the offering while Abraham carried the fire and the knife. Along the way, "Isaac spake unto Abraham his father, and said, My father: and he said, Here am I, my son. And he said, Behold the fire and the wood: but where is the lamb for a burnt offering?

And Abraham said, "My son, God will provide himself a lamb for a burnt offering: so they went both of them together."

Genesis 22:7-8 (KJV)

At the top of the mountain, Abraham built an altar, arranged the wood, and bound Isaac, laying him upon it. Just as he raised the knife to sacrifice his son, the angel of the Lord called out.

Transfiguration

"And the angel of the LORD called unto him out of heaven, and said, Abraham, Abraham: and he said, Here am I.

And he said, Lay not thine hand upon the lad, neither do thou any thing unto him: for now I know that thou fearest God, seeing thou hast not withheld thy son, thine only son from me."
Genesis 22:11-12 (KJV)

Abraham looked up and saw a ram caught in a thicket by its horns. God had indeed provided the sacrifice, just as Abraham had spoken in faith. He named that place Jehovah Jireh, meaning *"the Lord will provide."*

The story was never about Isaac being sacrificed.

It was about Abraham's willingness to surrender everything—even what he loved most—in obedience to God. And in that moment of surrender, God revealed His divine provision.

This is the essence of sacred submission. Surrendering our own will—our plans, our desires, our earthly attachments—is our proof that we are open to the miraculous provision God has for us. When we let go of what we think we need and want, God provides something far greater.

The day God asked me to give up my human desires in exchange for miracles, I received this message in my prayer corner:

—

As you sacrifice, I mend.
In your sacrifice, I magnify the healing powers that come from a broken heart.
In your submission of the natural man, I can call forth the powers

of your divine self.

Sacred submission is the center beam of the house of miracles.

—

We are not losing when we submit to God and align our body and soul with the Divine will. We are being transformed. We are being prepared for the miracles we were meant to receive. Every day, we have the opportunity to make this choice.

Each morning, may we ask:

What is God asking me to submit?

May today be the day we build our house of miracles, and may we build it upon the unshakable foundation of sacred submission.

Sacred Surrender

Sacred surrender is allowing yourself to fully surrender and release the struggles, the suffering, the pain, or the burden that you are carrying. This is the time to pick up your wounds, your broken heart, your financial struggles, and any other burdens that are weighing you down. It is here that you can ask for the help you need, and then trust that what you surrender can—and will—be transfigured.

Remember . . . when we sit with God, who we are at that time is magnified. And so it is in this moment that we activate the Law of Sacred Surrender so that we can be free from the weight we carry.

When we release, we receive.
When we surrender, we are strengthened.
And when we trust, miracles rain down upon us.

Transfiguration

The Washing of Mercy with Sacred Surrender + Submission

Since God abides by the **Law of Magnification,** whatever we bring to God is magnified. Because of this law, before I sit at the foot of God and ask for my daily blessing, I release what I do not want magnified. To do that, I must surrender everything that does not serve me.

This is where I pause. It is here that I pick up whatever struggle I am holding, whatever burden is weighing heavy, and I place it INTO God. I do not give it to God; I place it INTO God. For when it is placed INTO God, it immediately transforms by being within such Divine power.

Once I have done this, I ask, *"God, transfigure this. Take this burden from me and turn it into a miracle."*

And then I ask for mercy. I ask that the blessing of mercy will wash over my body, that the mercy of God will cleanse the burden, soothe the struggle, and lift the suffering from my being. I take a deep breath in and feel it leave, allowing myself to experience the relief of having that burden taken.

It is after the surrender that I get to choose the frequency I desire to be magnified. For once I have submitted my will, surrendered the pain, and asked for the washing of mercy to be poured over me, I am ready to ask for Christ to heal and transfigure me *down to my cells*. I am ready to become the energy and the vision that I want God to magnify.

And without the weight of such heavy burdens, this is now the time to move into the realm of full transfiguration.

CHAPTER 21

Re-coding Your Cells

One morning when I was deep in the inquiry of transfiguration, I was given these words in my daily blessing from God:

—

Within a single fingerprint of God lie all the codes needed for creation.
Ask to receive the fingerprint of God; ask that those codes move through you, reconfiguring the lines within your body and your system.

—

This idea may feel too simple: one fingerprint of God—and something in us shifts all the way down to our cells? Yet . . . I believe this to be true. What is within you calls forth the results outside of you.

At the root of your life are your cells; they script your patterns: reactions, thoughts, and ways of living. To become the miracle worker you're called to be, you must go all the way down to the cells.

But the truth is, your cells don't want to change. Their identity feels fixed. Day after day they follow predetermined programs. Some patterns are natural; others you inherited from your biological parents—many shaped by *their* traumas. Those patterns once kept you safe and brought you here, but many of them no longer serve you.

These patterns make true change feel nearly impossible. This is why you feel stuck in cyclical results, over and over. And this is why, when God calls you to fulfill a great vision, you want to run and hide. Your current set of cells tell you that what God has called you to do is impossible.

That is why transfiguration is essential for you to become WHO GOD HAS CALLED YOU TO BECOME. Your vision is impossible for the current cells and patterns running your body. The vision is calling forth a new pattern for your cells to follow. God's vision for you activates transfiguration.

But cells are like sheep. They follow patterns—what they've been taught, exposed to—and so those patterns repeat. This is the formula of patterns. Because of these patterns, it can feel like you are stuck. Yet, stuckness is an illusion, and you are a master creator.

This is when you ask Christ to imprint a new cellular pattern within you. By doing so, you give your cells a new blueprint to follow: a new energetic rhythm, a new divine instruction. This is the core of the Transfiguration Blessing. It is here that you will change.

No longer will old patterns be the master of your life. No more will you strive to bring God's vision to reality only to find yourself back in old stories—drowning in fear. No . . . everything changes now.

This is your Moses moment.

Let the vision that God has given you become the burning bush where YOU become transfigured. The vision has appeared; now you prepare the vessel that will carry it. We'll recode the cells to do just that.

Re-coding Your Cells

But before I recode my cells, I always prepare with the Blessing of the Body. I pour the water, activate the room, prepare the water, and cleanse the body. Think of a surgeon—the room is prepared, the instruments set, hands washed. That's what we're doing: preparing the space, the water, and the body.

This is the groundwork that lets our cells be transfigured. Preparation opens the door; surrender softens the fibers. Since our cells are loyal to what they've known, they cling to familiar loops. So we create a holy environment where a new blueprint can be received and held, where the body hears, *It's safe to change,* and begins to match the rhythm of miracles.

And I do not do this alone.

These blessings are not powered by me. They are not effective because I memorized the chakras or practiced energy healing. They carry power because of who I call in. And for me, that has always been Christ.

For years, I was trained in energy healing. I learned how to clear out the old and awaken the new within a person's body and energy field. I had protocols. Sequences. Hours of techniques designed to move energy and create healing. And they worked. But they took time.

One night, everything changed.

It was 2 a.m. I was lying next to my five-year-old son who was having nightmares. His mind was racing. His body was unsettled. I was exhausted. I began doing all the energy work I had been taught, cycling through each step to try and calm his nervous system and bring him peace. But it wasn't working fast enough. And I didn't have an hour to give.

A thought came: *Just ask Christ to come and heal him.*

Transfiguration

In my exhaustion, I did. Suddenly, what would have taken me an hour—Christ did in an instant. My son's body relaxed. His breathing slowed. His mind quieted. He fell asleep in peace. I lay there, stunned.

I had been raised Christian, but no one ever told me this was possible—that Christ was not just a distant God to worship from afar but a Teacher, a Presence I could call on, and a healing partner.

That night changed everything. From that moment on, I began working with Christ. Every blessing I offer—from my own body to the people I serve—is done in partnership with Him.

If "Christ" feels unfamiliar, you can call upon God, Source, Divine Light—but consider this: Christ is not distant. Christ is not reserved only for religion. You can sit with Christ and work with Him. He is available. He is willing. And He is here to partner with you in your transfiguration.

The Inner Becoming: Christ and the Cells

As Christ touched water and it became wine, Christ can touch your cells and transform them to match your vision. Since cells are stubborn about change but obedient to the pattern they're given, we clear the old, invite Christ to activate the new, and the cells follow with allegiance.

Any cells that will not transform slough off and die, leaving you only with cells aligned to the new design. This becomes the cellular re-coding within the Transfiguration Blessing.

There are two ways I guide this part of the blessing. You can ask that your cells match the frequency of miracles—the frequency of God. Or you can ask that your cells match the frequency of a specific vision God has shown you—whether it's a calling, a healing, a future, or a mission.

Re-coding Your Cells

When I began to experiment with this new concept, I received this message from God:

—

The rewiring is in the works and will be complete soon.
Move through the doubt; allow it to cleanse you so that your faith may sprout trust.
If Christ can touch water and it turns to wine, so can Christ change the frequency of your cells.
Deepen into this belief.

—

This is when I fully understood: if Christ could touch a blind man's eyes and open sight, or raise people from the dead, then I can ask Him to touch my cells and trust they will become new.

As I began to practice with this belief, God showed me that I needed to give Christ the visions I receive. The vision then becomes the new blueprint for my cells to follow. I then ask Christ to touch my cells and transform them to the frequency of this vision.

If I'm not working with a specific vision, I place the miracle I'm seeking into His hands and ask Him to encode it into my cellular patterns, down to the nucleus of every cell. I ask that any cells unable to receive this new blueprint gently slough off; I bless them, thank them for their service, and release them.

I ask that Christ will touch my cells so they may be activated and quickened to a higher frequency. I ask that the blueprint of *(insert your vision here)*—or the blueprint of miracles—be activated within me. I ask that Christ will activate my brain patterns to rewire and align with this frequency so that every thought, every cell, and every part of my being matches the energy of this vision.

Transfiguration

—

I then take three deep breaths to allow this process to take place. As I breathe, I visualize the activation and feel the rewiring begin. And when it is complete . . .

—

I ask that any cells not aligned with this pattern will slough off gently and be released—with gratitude. I thank them for their service. And I let them go.

—

> Here is an example for you to experiment with. Use this first and then create your own:
>
> Christ, I have surrendered my will, my problems, and my desires to God.
>
> Here is the vision God has given me (or: here is the miracle I seek).
>
> Touch my cells and transform them to match the frequency of this vision.
>
> Please activate my brain patterns to rewire and align with this frequency
>
> so that every thought, every cell, and every part of my being matches the energy of this vision.
>
> Encode this instruction into my cellular patterns—down to the nucleus of every cell.
>
> And if any cell cannot receive this new design, let it gently slough off. I bless it, I thank it for its service, and I release it in gratitude.

Re-coding Your Cells

It is here and now that you begin to fully rise. Rise into the newness of who you were always meant to be. This is the rebirth of you and your work. For the cells that have held you back have died, and the cells that have stayed have become new in and through the power of Christ.

The blueprint of your vision has been awakened and embedded down to the core of your being. Take a deep breath in and allow yourself to feel different. The chains have been released, and the freedom from the old ways has now been birthed.

You are new.

CHAPTER 22

DNA Transfiguration

When my body is anointed and my chakra centers are activated through the blessing—after I have submitted my will and surrendered my burdens into God, and Christ has tuned my cells to the frequency of the vision or the miracle I am seeking—I go deeper.

This is the transfiguration of the DNA.

I was taught this practice through the holy parable of the olive tree. One morning I was brought to the parable of the Olive Tree, which can be found in two different holy texts:

Romans 11:17–24 — God grafts wild olive branches into the cultivated tree and can graft the natural branches back in.

Jacob 5 (The Book of Mormon) — In this extended Allegory of the Olive Tree, branches of the tree are cut, moved, grafted, and nourished until the new tree becomes one.

I was shown that what God does with the branches in the parable, He can do with codes within us—*down to the very strands of our DNA.*

That morning, I saw a vision so clearly: it was a grafting of DNA strands. I was shown that we can ask Christ to lift out the DNA thread of an old pattern, belief, or behavior that no longer serves us. As He pulls it out, the code dissolves in the presence of Divine light. Then we can ask Christ to graft in a thread of His DNA code—the strand that matches the vision or miracle we seek.

After I ask for this to be done, I sit in quiet awareness and breathe deeply into the vision of my DNA codes accepting the graft. I sit until my body recalibrates to this new frequency. And just like the parables above, the graft becomes complete and I am one with Christ. And I am one with God.

This is the full transfiguration.

This is the moment you step out of old patterns and into a new frequency. This is where transformation takes place—not just spiritually but biologically. And it is here that you are now the frequency that you desire to have magnified as you sit at the foot of God.

Now that you match the frequency you want, the Law of Magnification activates and produces the miracles you desire.

The Daily Blessing

This is the moment where I ask that this Transfiguration will be sealed with a blessing. I ask that God, Christ, and the Divine Mother will come and place their hands on my head. And then I ask Them to give me a blessing—a message, guidance, an answer, the exact words I need for that day.

This is a custom blessing I receive every single day.

Transfiguration

After I ask, I listen. I take a few minutes to be still. I don't usually see anything. I don't always hear anything. But when I open my prayer journal and put my pen to the paper, words are given. Words I didn't know. Words that are for me. Words that heal me. Words that remind me that I am known.

Even in a sea of billions of people—God knows me. God hears me. God speaks to me.

This is my favorite part of the entire blessing because this is where I sit with God. This is where I hear God. This is where I become new.

And I want you to know: you can receive this too.

I invite you to call upon whomever you feel comfortable with: God, Christ, Divine Mother, the angels, your ancestors, the Presence you know and love. Ask for a blessing. Ask to be held. Ask to hear.

I have sat with hundreds of people and taught them this. And everyone hears.

It is not just a hope. It is a law, a law written in every holy text across every sacred tradition: when you ask—*you will receive.*

God did not stop speaking to humans centuries ago. God did not die with the Bible. Those miracles ceased because we lost the belief that God speaks to us and that we can speak to God.

You do not need someone to hear from God for you. As you prepare like the prophets of old did, and create the sacred within yourself, you can sit at the foot of God and hear—hear what God's voice says for you.

If there is one thing that I know deeper than anything, it is this: *if you ask, you will receive. Ask to hear God, and you will.*

DNA Transfiguration

The heavens will open.

I believe we are here to keep the heavens open. And as we do this work, we call forth the fire from heaven just like Elijah of old did.

Devotion is the path.

When your room is cleansed and consecrated, your centers are blessed, your cells are re-coded, and your DNA grafted to match the frequency of Christ, you become new. New in every part of you—your mind, your heart, your soul, your cells, even your DNA.

Transfiguration is a completion of the old and a renewal of the newness that is offered and yours to have.

For you: you were called to build worlds—worlds that are weaved by the very threads of miracles, worlds that are held together by love, worlds where light rests upon our eyelashes and washes our sight so that we may see as God sees.

Here is the order and an example of the Transfiguration Blessing:

Cleanse and Prepare Your Room

I ask that Christ will touch the walls, the floors, the doors, the windows, and anything and everything that is in this room that it will be cleansed and cleaned. I then ask that Christ will touch each part of this room that it will be magnified and activated to match the frequency of miracles.

Transfiguration

Call in your Angels and Guides
I ask that God will call in all of my angels and guides in and through the Divine light to hold me in safety and love.

Bless the Water and then Bless the Body
This is where you refer back to "The Sacred Centers" chapter and bless the chakras of your body.

Place your burdens and your will into God with the blessing of sacred surrender and submission.
"God, I place INTO you my burdens (name them), my will (name it), and my struggles. Please transfigure them to match the frequency of miracles."

Ask Christ to touch your cells to match the blueprint of your vision or the frequency of miracles.
"Christ, I have surrendered my will, my problems, and my desires to God.
Here is the vision God has given me (or: here is the miracle I seek).
I ask that you touch my cells and transform them to match the frequency of this vision.
Please activate my brain patterns to rewire and align with this frequency
so that every thought, every cell, and every part of my being matches the energy of this vision.
Encode this instruction into my cellular patterns, down to the nucleus of every cell.
And if any cell cannot receive this new design, let it gently

DNA Transfiguration

slough off. I bless it, I thank it for its service, and I release it in peace."

I ask that Christ will pull out the thread of DNA that I desire to have transfigured and then replace it by grafting in a thread of Christ's DNA code.

"Christ—I ask that you go within the very threads of my DNA code and pull out the DNA strand of (name the patterns CLEARLY). I ask that this code disintegrate within the presence of Divine light. I ask that you, Christ, will now graft in a thread of your DNA. The thread that matches (name what you desire to match your vision or the frequency of miracles). I ask that my DNA coding may become One with God, as you are."

I ask for a blessing to seal this work with.

I ask that God, Divine Mother, and Christ may place their hands on my head to give me a blessing. Seal this transfiguration up with love and peace. And please give me the words that I need today.

Then place your pen to a page in your prayer book, listen, and receive God's word for you.

Transfiguration

PART V
LIVING AS A PROPHET

Transfiguration

> A prophet or prophetess is one who feels the call . . . seeks . . . and desires to KNOW God.
> To hear God.
>
> Prepares to sit at the foot of God and receives.
> They write God's words and bring them to the world.
> They teach truth and allow it to land as it needs to.
>
> To live as a prophet requires faith, strength, determination. and surrender.

CHAPTER 23

Learning to Live after Transfiguration

You have prepared your body. You have learned how to surrender your will. You have matched your cells to the frequency of your vision. You have asked Christ to transfigure you. And something has already changed.

You may not have language for it yet. You may not fully trust it. But you can feel it. There is a subtle shift inside you now, a quiet discomfort with the way things used to be. The rhythms that once felt normal may suddenly feel tight. The routines that once grounded you may no longer satisfy you.

This is not because something is wrong. It is because you are no longer the same.

This is the part no one really teaches: how do you live in the world after God has altered your frequency?

You don't leave your life behind. You still wake up. You still go to work. You still raise children. You still move through ordinary days. But you are not living ordinarily anymore.

Transfiguration

Once you have been transfigured, monotony becomes painful. Miracles are the end of monotony, and the path of the prophet is paved with the stones of miracles. Miracles happen when we leave the realm of sameness.

Monotony is the thief of creation. It's the chains we opt into again and again, worshipping our limitations as if they'll protect us. But the truth is—monotony is our greatest enemy. It is here that we watch our lives pass us by, not as creators but as viewers. It is the lie we keep feasting on, hoping that somehow it will taste different next time.

REBEL against this sameness. BREAK FREE from the chains of monotony. And choose instead to create with vision and weave miracles.

That's why we call them miracles . . . because they interrupt the cycle. They pull us out of the predictable, the dull, and the forgettable. They wake us up.

Because to be human is to be wrapped in forgetfulness, and monotony is the lullaby that lulls us into forgetting. Every time we walk the same path, think the same thoughts, live the same patterns—we fall asleep again. And here's the most dangerous part: we start to believe we are alive . . . when we're really just dreaming of life.

But miracles require an awakening. And this is the life of a prophet.

To live the life of a prophet or prophetess, you must demand miracles. And to do so, you must remember who YOU ARE. Once you remember who you are, forgetting no longer feels peaceful. It feels dissonant.

You may find yourself longing for the simplicity of life as it was before your calling—before the visions, before the responsibility of faith, before God asked you to move mountains. This longing is human. And it is also the lure.

Learning to Live after Transfiguration

You can remember who you were. You can love who you were. You can grieve who you were. But you cannot live there again. Just as I cannot fit into the clothes I wore at five years old, you cannot return to who you were before God awakened you. Trying to will suffocate you.

And as you live this way, something else might happen that can feel unsettling at first. Certain people will no longer be able to stay in your life—not because you stopped loving them, not because you rejected them, but because your frequency has changed. Light burns what cannot be held.

Some relationships will fall away. Some dynamics will collapse. Some conversations will no longer fit. This isn't punishment. It's resonance.

Your life may feel quieter, lonelier, less familiar. But know that nothing has gone wrong. This is not a sign that you misheard God. This is not proof that you are too much. This is not a failure of love. It is the natural rearranging that happens when truth begins to lead.

So how do you live as a prophet in the world when your life no longer looks the same, when you feel different, when you no longer fit where you once did?

You return. Every day. You open your palms. You sit with God. And you ask: *What is the most important action I take today?*

Even when you feel misunderstood. Even when you are walking alone. Even when your visions are questioned by others, or by yourself—you still go. You still sit. You still ask. You still listen. And then—*you do.*

This is the rhythm of a prophet's life.

You live by demanding miracles: not someday, not when things calm down, not when life feels aligned. Every day. You claim them. You match them. You live as though God is active now.

Transfiguration

Because God is.

This is not arrogance. This is devotion. A prophet does not wait for permission to believe.

As you live this way, God will give you more visions. And those visions will become your line of sight. They will guide your decisions, anchor your faith, and steady you when nothing else makes sense.

Your visions become your North Star.

You will stop merely surviving. You will begin to thrive.

And remember—gone are the days when prophets must be destroyed to be heard. Gone are the days when prophets must disappear to be powerful. Now is the time that prophets and prophetesses live.

Now is the time your voice becomes a beacon. Now is the time your faith lights the way for others. Now is the time you claim your place—not above humanity but within it—as a leader of God.

You are not here to shrink. You are not here to hide. You are not here to remember quietly.

You are here to lead.
You are here to speak.
You are here to remind the world.

This is how you live as a prophet—not apart from life, but fully awake within it.

And now . . .
Now is your time.

CHAPTER 24

The Persecution of the Prophets, and, Disrupt Anyway . . .

There will be times when you want to run away to a cave. The path is lonely, and a lot of people might not like you. You disrupt because the truth disrupts established patterns within humans. These patterns feel safe for most people, and so they will guard them.

This is why, when you speak truth, it might make people angry. It will enrage them. It will make them want you to go away. And you were made for this.

There may be times when even your closest friends desert you. But know this: it isn't you they are deserting. It isn't you they dislike. It is the truth you've been called to speak. It is your faith that shakes the walls of their fear. It is your actions that crack the foundation of their doubt. It is your love that burns through the illusions they've made a home in.

Transfiguration

Illusions feel safe—not because they are true, but because they are familiar. People know how to function inside their illusions. But when you shine truth on these illusions, they disintegrate. This leaves people with nothing to cling to: no stories, no scapegoats, no structure for supporting them through their fears.

This is the disruption you'll create.

But here's the gift: As you step forward as a leader, as people throw hate at you or speak poorly of you, you get to choose love. You get to understand that it's not about you. And if it's not about you, then the deeper question becomes: how will *you* show up in love?

How will you see these people—not as persecutors, but as children needing love? How do you respond when they hate you because your truth threatens the belief that they are powerless?

You do it by loving them like the mother they wish they had. By witnessing them like the father they never knew. You do it by being one who sees them—even as they throw stones at you.

Because this—this is the real disruption.
Love is the ultimate disruptor.

People will reject, ridicule, and persecute you for seeing, telling, and acting on the truth. And the most disruptive truth you can stand for is love.

I know how hard this is to hear, because you are still human. And no one likes being disliked, hated, gossiped about. No one. You are not an ascended master—yet. You are filled with flaws and weaknesses. You still make mistakes.

The Persecution of the Prophets, and, Disrupt Anyway . . .

So when people come against you, it's easy to question everything—question your gifts, question your path—to want to give up, to want to run back to the cave.

But if you do, you forfeit this beautiful, wild experiment that life offers you. And most of all, you forfeit the opportunity to walk in divine love.

God gave me this vision on a day that I was questioning my own gifts:

—

Your belief is your superpower.
When you stop believing—everything ends.

There was once a woman with firepower. Her whole life, she built fires—for warmth, for cooking, for comfort. She served, she gave, she built. One day, she discovered someone had attached a firestarter to her arms. What she once believed was her innate gift, it turned out, was rigged all along.

Instead of feeling empowered, she ran to a cave. She lived in bitterness and in doubt. But what she didn't understand was this: it didn't matter how the fire came. It mattered that she used it for good.

The firestarter in someone else's hands could have caused destruction. But she was chosen because of her heart. She was given fire because God knew what she would do with it.

—

This is the same for you. Your gift is your heart. And it doesn't matter how you got your gifts. It doesn't matter if you don't even like your gifts. What matters is how you use them.

So don't run to the cave. Don't give up. Continue walking in love, even when it feels unreciprocated.

Transfiguration

Yes—prophets are persecuted. But if you stay in love, be in love, you will still disrupt anyway, and you will stay in peace.

Let people talk. Let them throw stones. Let them doubt. You—disrupt anyway. Disrupt with your joy. Disrupt with your presence. Disrupt with your fierce obedience. Disrupt with your peace. Disrupt with your tenderness. Disrupt with your love.

Because love is the most powerful miracle of all.

God showed me something new—something that shifted everything. If we are the holy disruption—and we are—then persecution is inevitable. All prophets and prophetesses have been disruptors. They disturbed comfort. They interrupted illusions. They exposed the places people were hiding in.

But here's what God said to me: *you get to choose whether or not you are persecuted.*

If you take offense, if you believe their anger is about you, if you internalize their fear or shrink in response to their projections, then you are choosing to be persecuted.

But they don't hate you. They don't fear you. They are just resisting what you carry. Because truth breaks patterns. Truth shatters illusions. Truth invites people to see themselves clearly. And there is no higher truth than love.

And love breaks illusions.

Most people are not ready for that. They worship their patterns—even if they're painful—because they're familiar. They understand the illusion because they can predict it.

But when you show up in the fullness of who you are, when you speak truth in love, when you carry the presence of God—that challenges them. It exposes the illusions they've built their lives around. It asks them to become something they've never believed they could be.

They persecute you to defend these illusions. You can't change that. You can only choose your response.

And here's your holy choice: will you become a victim and martyr... or will you choose to become love?

God told me:

—

People are angry because they have never been heard.
People are cruel because they have never been seen.

But if you can be Presence...

If you can see them with the eyes of God...

If you can witness them in their sacred becoming...
Love will dissolve the rage.

This is the power of love.

—

When you remember who you are, you don't resist opposition; you transcend it. You don't collapse; you anchor. When you truly live in your divine identity, when you embody your calling with no apology, slander can't touch you. Judgment can't shake you. Hate can't move you.

Because your frequency is love.

Christ, in His final moments, was the embodiment of this truth. And even as He was being crucified, He looked at the very people who betrayed Him and said:

Transfiguration

"Father, forgive them; for they know not what they do." Luke 23:34 (KJV)

That is the highest disruption. That is how we keep going. That is how we keep loving.
That is how we keep performing miracles.

So yes . . . they may talk. They may turn away. They may not understand.

Disrupt anyway.
Lead anyway.
Love anyway.

Because you are the miracle.

CHAPTER 25

Live as the Prophet Now

This is how you live as a prophet now: not by chasing miracles, not by clinging to outcomes, but by learning how to stay awake, faithful, and aligned after God moves.

This chapter is not about getting miracles. It is about how you live once they arrive.

After witnessing a miracle, it is easy to forget. This happens when we become so fixated on the outcome that we lose sight of what actually happened. We long for miracles because we believe they will make us feel different—more whole, more at peace, more fulfilled. But the truth is, feeling different doesn't come from the miracle itself. *It comes from within us.*

We expect miracles to change how we feel. When that expectation is not met, we often discount or discredit the miracle itself. Instead of recognizing what has already occurred, we begin searching for the next miracle, hoping it will finally change us. But miracles do not change us.

We change us.

Transfiguration

Often, when God calls us into a larger vision, we follow it believing that once it is achieved, once it is built, accomplished, or created—then the joy, peace, and fulfillment we have been seeking will finally arrive.

This is the trap of the prophet, the trap that can take even the most powerful leader and slowly turn them into a victim of their own calling.

Many who are called become victims of their callings because they follow inspiration with an expectation of how it should feel.

And when they perform the miracle, build the empire, create with God, and still struggle, they turn and blame the very God who called them.

When we expect God to save us in a particular way, and the imagined results of our visions do not arrive, we turn our expectations into chains.

This is especially dangerous for prophets because returning to normalcy is no longer an option. They have come too far to turn back. And when the calling or vision leaves them feeling overwhelmed, broken, or burdened, they begin to feel imprisoned by the very God they love.

But it was never promised that speaking truth, creating miracles, or carrying revelation would bring constant peace or comfort. To recognize this, and to live awake inside of it, is the daily work of a prophet.

One morning, God's words led me into a deeper understanding of this truth:

Live as the Prophet Now

—

Wonder is the way.
Stay in wonder.
Be in wonder.
Allow wonder.
Speak wonder.

—

The prophet eventually learns this: how they feel is not God's responsibility, nor the calling's, nor the miracle's. God calls, God reveals, and God moves, but the prophet chooses how they meet what unfolds.

When wonder is protected, when awe is practiced rather than replaced by expectation; joy remains available even as the calling intensifies, even as pressure increases, even as persecution arises.

Gratitude is not something the prophet waits to feel after the breakthrough; it is something they learn to feel inside the weight, inside the resistance, and inside the cost.

And when a prophet can remain grateful while misunderstood, joyful while being stretched, and awake while carrying the full gravity of their assignment, that is arrival.

Arrival is not a destination. It is a way of feeling.

And this—the capacity to remain alive, present, and grateful in the midst of the calling—is how a prophet lives to the fullest measure of their life.

This is the most important moment in a prophet's life. Not the moment they first heard God. Not the moment they chose to act. Not even the moment they became the miracle worker. It is this moment—the

Transfiguration

moment they choose how they will live inside the calling they have already received.

It is the moment they choose peace, even in the face of pressure, fear, overwhelm, and intensity. The moment they choose joy, even if they did everything God asked and still find themselves emptied, misunderstood, or standing in the aftermath of obedience without the reward they imagined.

In that moment, the prophet does not wait to be made happy. They choose how they will feel, *despite everything*.

This is where prophets live.

Not in certainty and not in comfort but *in wonder*. They do not wait for peace to arrive once the work is finished; they learn how to feel it while carrying the work itself. They do not postpone joy until the vision is fulfilled; they discover how to remain alive and grateful while becoming the person capable of holding it.

This is the quiet mastery of a prophet: the ability to remain present and devoted without demanding that God make the path easier, clearer, or more familiar. There is nothing more required now, no final striving, no last effort to prove worthiness. There is only consent—the willingness to trust, to allow, and to live as though what has been promised is already in motion.

Because it is.

The miracle you are waiting for is not somewhere ahead of you; it meets you in the way you choose to walk forward from here, when you stop asking for proof, not because doubt has vanished, but because trust has taken its place.

This is the moment that determines everything.

This is the moment you become free.

Not because the calling disappears, but because you no longer run from it. This is the moment you stop chasing miracles and stop arguing with the vision, when you no longer need to know how, yet you still walk forward and become.

You move without scrambling, without bargaining, without trying to manage what was never yours to control. And in that quiet steadiness, you realize you are no longer trying to keep pace with God—*you are walking beside God.*

There is no stumbling now, no grasping, no fear of falling behind. Only the sovereign knowing that you are already moving at the stride of the One who called you.

This is the path of Transfiguration.

Transfiguration

ADDENDUM

BLESSINGS FROM THE PRAYER CORNER

Every day, I meet with God and practice the Transfiguration Blessing. What follows are blessings that were spoken in real time, in living communion with God. These were not written after the fact or refined later. They were recorded as I sat in my prayer corner and listened.

These words are not meant to be studied. They are meant to be received.

Let one blessing meet you. Sit with it. Breathe. Allow your body to soften before your mind tries to understand. There is no rush here.

And remember this: *I do not receive* for *you.*

These blessings are not a replacement for your own communion with God. They are a reminder of it.

God still speaks; and God speaks to you.

Transfiguration

You do not need to become more ready. You do not need to wait for a more sacred moment. There is no place more holy than where you are now. There is no time more open than this one.

Let these words open the space.

Then ask, listen, and do.

I.

Daily Entry Blessings

The Fast Version of the Blessing:

This is the blessing I do every day at lunch and sometimes before bed. This is a blessing to do when you only have a few minutes.

—-

Take a nice deep breath in from the crown of the head, letting it move all the way down the body and out through the soles of the feet.

I ask that Christ will come and bless this water: that it will be cleaned, cleansed, and cleared all the way down to the molecules; that the molecules of the water may match the frequency of the molecular structure of miracles.

I ask that Christ will bless my crown chakra, my third eye, my eyes, my ears, my nose, and my lips. I ask that Christ will bless my throat chakra, the back of my head, C7, and my nervous system.

I ask that Christ will bless my front heart and my back heart, my front solar plexus and my back solar plexus. I ask that Christ will bless my navel and my sacral and my root chakras.

Transfiguration

I ask that Christ may bless my arms and my hands, that they may be God's hands. I ask that Christ may bless my feet, that they may be God's feet.

I then ask for a full blessing of peace to rest upon my body. I ask that love may move throughout every cell inside of me and that fear has no part within.

I take a deep breath in, and I ask that light may shield and protect my being, that the path in front of me may be shown, that I may be guided . . . and directed on this very day.

Thank you. Thank you. Thank you.

―――

The Blessing of the Body:

This is the chakra blessing. This is a blessing I do when I have fifteen minutes to pray. This is also a blessing I often do right before I sleep.

―――

I take a deep breath in, allowing divine light to move through my body from the crown of the head all the way down to the tips of my toes. I call in all of my angels and my guides, through the Divine Light, that they may come and sit with me, that they may show me exactly what needs to come through today, that they may hold me in safety and peace, that they may partner with me in my work.

I ask that Christ may pour light through the palms of my hands and touch this water, that this water may be cleaned, cleansed, and cleared, and that it may be activated to match the frequency of God, to match the frequency of miracles. I ask that Christ may bless my crown chakra, that my crown chakra may be opened, that I may receive from God today; that the channels may be clear, and that the Divine Light may move through my whole entire being, cleaning me out, cleaning out anyone's energy that does not serve me, cleaning all the fear out of my body, for it has no place or part within me.

I breathe in, and I breathe out.

I ask that Christ may bless my third eye, that my gifts may be cleaned, that my gifts may be claimed, that I claim them, and that I partner with them, that they participate in my mission and my work with me. And I ask that the Divine Mother may kiss my third eye, that Her love—a love that is boundless, a love with no condition, a love that exceeds love beyond time and space—may move through my pituitary gland. And as this love moves through this gland, that Her love may become the commanding center for every cell, that every cell in my body may move at the frequency of such love.

I breathe in, and I breathe out.

I ask that Christ may cleanse my eyes, that whatever I have been blind to, whatever I have not seen, whatever I refuse to see, may be shown to me; that truth may be the line of sight of my eyes; that I may see truth everywhere, and that I may see truth and live truth and be truth; and that I may see the miracles that God has given me.

I breathe in, and I breathe out.

I ask that Christ may bless my nose, that I may receive: that I may receive abundance, that I may receive love, that I may receive ease, that I may receive joy, that I may receive miracles as easily as it is for me to receive this breath through my nose. I ask that Christ may bless my ears, that my ears may be cleaned and cleansed and cleared, that they may be unclogged, and that my hearing may be heightened physically, and that my spiritual hearing may be heightened to match

Transfiguration

the frequency of the voice of God, that I might hear God as God speaks to me.

I breathe in, and I breathe out.

Ask that Christ may bless my lips, that they may be washed, cleaned, and cleared; that all of the things that I have ever said that were not of light may be cleared from my being; and that I may only speak truth, that I may speak my dreams into reality, that I may speak my visions into worlds, that my words build miracles, and that my lips may be anointed to meet with God.

I breathe in, and I breathe out.

I asked that Christ may bless the back of my head, that the back of my head may be cleaned and cleansed and cleared, and that I may release the patterns: the cyclical patterns, the fears, the doubts, and the loops that have held me in my old shapes—the loops that have called in behaviors, called in the wrong people, called in the wrong opportunities—everything that has looped me into these lower vibrations, that they may be cleared out of my body . . . from here, evermore; and that truth may move through the back of my head, that truth becomes the loop that loops through my being, that truth is the rhythm of my body, that truth is the rhythm of cells, that truth aligns me to match with God.

I breathe in, and I breathe out.

I ask that Christ will bless C7—my nervous system—that it may be nourished with the deepest energy of love; that my nervous system may be held, that it may be swaddled, that it may be seen, that it may be held in the deepest place of peace; and that any inspiration that I have refused to take action on that has created such burnout and overwhelm may be cleared from my being so that I may be able to take action. And as I take action—action that is inspired—my nervous system is activated with the deepest energy of nourishment and love, for inspired action is what tunes my nervous system to match the frequency of God.

I breathe in, and I breathe out.

I ask that Christ will bless my throat chakra that my voice may be liberated, that I may speak the truths I have been given, that I may speak truth, that I may speak truths into existence, that I may speak truths into my own being, that truth may run through my body and that my voice may be liberated and uncapped; that my voice may reach the edges of the earth that I may speak the words that God has called me to speak; and that I may allow others to see and hear me in my power, in my truth, in my wonder, and in my joy.

I breathe in, and I breathe out.

I ask that Christ may bless my front heart chakra that it may be soft, that it may be open, that I may receive: that I may receive the wonders of heaven, that I may receive deep love, that I may receive the miracles that God has for me, and that I may be a conduit of such divine love. That I may give as God gives, that I may love as God loves, and that I may bring God's love down to this earth in physical form, that my heart may be the receptacle of such peace, of such love, of such wonder.

I breathe in, and I breathe out.

I ask that Christ may bless my back heart, that my back heart may be blessed and washed with the law of mercy, with the blessing of mercy, and with the law of forgiveness that I may forgive: that I may forgive those who have hurt me, that I may forgive those who have abused me, that I may forgive those who have harmed me. That I may forgive, and I may be blessed with the blessing of mercy so that bitterness and resentment may leave my body; they have no place or role here. I ask

Transfiguration

that unconditional love may be the source of my back heart—love that has no condition, a love that exceeds my wildest dreams—may it pulse through my being, may it heal my back heart wounds, and may it make my heart soft so that I may receive more from God.

I breathe in, and I breathe out.

I ask that Christ may bless my front solar plexus. Bless it that I may take action on all that God has inspired me to do. May the doors be opened to the paths that have been paved that I may lift my foot and that I may walk.

I ask that the breath of life be poured into my front solar plexus, that this fire may always be burning, and that as I take action, I may move at the stride of God.

I breathe in, and I breathe out.

I ask that Christ will bless my back solar plexus that all of my victim energy, that all of my fear, that all of my terror, that all of my doubt may dissipate within the presence of God; and that every weave of victim energy may be pulled from the corners and the edges of my body, that every ounce of fear that has been held within my being may be vacuumed from within the very nucleus of every cell, and that Christ may clear this from my being. That Christ may place his hand upon my back solar plexus, encoding within the blessings of—the blessings of the priestess, the priest, the queen, the king, the blessing of the one who walks and talks with God, the one who can turn fear into faith, the one who can alchemize doubt into trust, the one who can magnify the blessings of miracles. May this be placed within my back solar plexus, for here and evermore—reaching the corners and the edges of my skin, reaching the corners and the edges of the universe—making me one with God.

I breathe in, and I breathe out.

Ask that Christ may bless my naval chakra, that it may be cleaned, cleansed, and cleared, that I may surrender all of my attachments—all my attachments to the desires that I have, the dreams that I have, the wants that I have—that I may surrender them over to God. And in sacred submission, I ask that God will bless me with the higher path, that I may see as God sees and that I may connect into God. And I surrender over my burdens. I surrender over my will, my fears, my terrors, my pains, my traumas, my suffering, my attachment to suffering, my attachment to abuse, my attachment to wounds, and ask that God may cleanse these out of my body, that they have no place or part within me anymore—cleaning me out completely here and forever. And I ask that I may be plugged into the One—the One who sees, the One who knows, the One who loves—that I may be plugged into the love of the Divine Mother, the love of God, the healing of Christ, and that I may be in the deepest place of wholeness.

I breathe in, and I breathe out.

I ask that Christ may bless my sacral chakra, that I may love myself as God loves me; that this love for who I am is deeper than eternity, that this love goes deeper than the very cells of my body, that this love races through my veins as the blood that pumps through the heart of my being, that I may be love and that love may be me; and as so the passion within my being may be activated, so that the passion is used for good, so that the passion is used for co-creation with God; and that I and God become one—co-creators and partners of a world that heals, that has been made whole.

I breathe in, and I breathe out.

I ask that Christ may bless my root chakra that abundance may pulse through the very being of who I am; that the truth of abundance, the truth of who God is—that God is abundance—pours through me: just as there is always enough oxygen, there are always enough trees, there

Transfiguration

are always enough leaves, there are always enough flowers, there is always enough water in the ocean—for God's deepest truth is abundance.

And I ask for this truth to be the code that is placed within my root, that abundance pulses through me and that the lies and illusions of lack may dissipate, for they have no truth; I ask that they may be gone. I ask that God may touch my root chakra, and encode me with the fingerprint of God—the fingerprint of abundance, the fingerprint of wonder, the fingerprint of all. May it be done now.

I breathe in, and I breathe out.

And I ask that Christ may bless my arms and my hands that they may be God's hands. I ask that Christ may bless my feet, that my feet may be God's feet, that I may serve as God, and that I may walk as God, and that I may hold the sacred, *sacred,* from within my very being; and that every place in which I stand, **I create the Holy.** I activate the remembrance and ask that my feet may be coded with the directions of where I am going, that they may have the maps from within them to lead me on the path that God has paved, that I may be one with God and that God may be one with me.

I breathe in, and I breathe out.

And today, I seal this blessing up, and I ask for this to be held in gratitude, to be held in love, to be held in light. And I ask that God, Christ, and the Divine Mother may place their hands upon my head, that I may receive a blessing—the blessing that is for me today, the blessing that I may receive here and now.

I open my palms and I listen.

Thank you. Thank you. Thank you.

II.

Transfiguration Blessings

The Full Transfiguration Blessing:

This is the full Transfiguration Blessing. This includes the blessing of the body, the cellular re-coding, and the DNA grafting. I do this full blessing every morning.

—

I take a deep breath in from the crown of my head, and I ask that God may pour His love through me like an ocean, moving and ebbing throughout the very corners and edges of my body, all the way down to the tips of my toes, recalibrating me to once again remember God, to once again feel the presence of God above me, below me, around me, and within me: that I am God and God is me, and that we are held together in this love. I ask that we partner this morning in this work.

I call in all of the armies of angels—those who have been assigned to me in my work. I ask that they may come and sit with me, that they may participate, and that they may support me now and throughout the day, that pathways may be opened, that doors may be unveiled, that windows be unleashed. For I am here to sit at the foot of God, to

Transfiguration

participate in the blessing of the transfiguration, and I ask for their help in this work.

And I ask that Christ may touch this water, that it will be cleaned, cleansed, and cleared down to the molecular structure; that it may match the frequency of the molecules of miracles, that it may match the frequency of God. I take this water, and I ask that Christ may bless my crown chakra, that my crown may be healed, that all the resistance I have had toward God may be cleared, that instead I may open the crown, that I may hear God, that as I sit with God today, the voice of God moves through me like a rhythm, like a heartbeat of my very soul. And that I may receive as I was called to receive. **May this be so.**

I breathe in, and I breathe out.

I ask that Christ may bless my third eye, that Christ may cleanse the cobwebs from off of the gifts that I have refused to use, that Christ may awaken them that they may become new in and through Christ; that my gifts may claim their territory within me and that I may partner with my gifts as they were created to be, that I may use them as God uses gifts, and that I may claim them as the queen that I am; and that these gifts may move with me like the breath that I breathe, like the steps that I take, like the songs that I sing, *that they are one within me now.*

I ask that the Divine Mother may place Her love within my third eye with a kiss of love—a love that reminds me of who I am, a love that brings me into wholeness—and that this love may be the commander of my cells, that my cells may know the frequency of divine love, and that they may follow this blueprint; that the space within my being may be shielded, protected, and held in peace.

I breathe in, and I breathe out.

Transfiguration Blessings

I ask that Christ may bless my eyes, that my eyes may be anointed—to have the blindness of humanity cleansed—and that the sight of divinity may be awakened within the very eyes that are within me that I may see the world as God sees it, that I may see the opportunities as God sees them, that I may see and witness the miracles that God has given me now.

I breathe in, and I breathe out.

I ask that Christ may bless my nose, that my senses may be activated, that my senses may ground me into this present time—into the present time of being human—and that my senses may connect me to my humanity and my divinity; that I may receive miracles as simply as it is to receive the blessings: the blessing of breath and the blessings of peace. May I receive them now.

I ask that Christ may bless my ears, that my ears may be protected, that my ears may be unclogged, and that I may hear as God hears. I ask that Christ may touch my ears so that they may be tuned to the frequency of the voice of God—so that I may hear God now and throughout today, in every pocket and in every way. I ask that the voice of God may be the base rhythm of my life, that I may hear the messages that God has for me—with ease.

I breathe in, and I breathe out.

I ask that Christ may bless my lips, that they will be washed, cleansed, and anointed to speak with God today. I bless my lips that they may speak the words that God has anointed me to speak on this planet, that I may bring truth to humanity, and that as I speak, I build new worlds—worlds that are based on faith, worlds that are built off of hope, belief, and trust; worlds that are weaved together with miracles.

I breathe in, and I breathe out.

Transfiguration

I ask that Christ may bless the back of my head. I ask that Christ will place His hands on the back of my head to bless it with the energy of safety, letting me know that it is safe to release my old patterns—allowing my body to feel grounded in releasing the old ways and the old beliefs. I ask that Christ may pour so much love through the back of my head that the lies and illusions that have run my system will be swaddled in this love, and in the swaddling they will dissipate. I ask that Christ may pulse truth through my being, that truth may loop through me, that truth may pierce to the very core of who I am, activating the brilliance that has always been within.

I breathe in, and I breathe out.

I ask that Christ may place golden nectar into my C7 and nervous system—first cleansing it and flushing it—that all the burnout that is within my body may be cleared, and that the nourishment of divine love will move through every nerve within my being; that it will move to the very edges of the nerves, and as it goes in, it brings the nerves to a place of peace. This love brings the nerves into a place of grounded rest. And then I ask that Christ will tune my nervous system to match the frequency of God so that I may sit in the presence of God longer.

I breathe in, and I breathe out.

I ask that Christ may bless my throat chakra, that first it may be healed—healed from all the times that my voice was clamped; that I may be healed from all the times that I was told to play small, to be small, to be quiet, to stay still. And in forgiveness, I release them, and I ask that Christ may open the doors and free my voice, liberate my messages, allow me to see myself and hear myself as God does—and in the doing, that I may allow others to hear me and see me as God does.

I breathe in, and I breathe out.

I ask that Christ may bless my front heart, that it may be cleaned and cleansed and cleared; that all the pain that has ever found its way in—all the broken glass, all the brokenness, all the betrayal, all the rejection—I ask that Christ may clear it out now; and that through the fire of Christ's love, all the broken glass may be molded into creation. And in this creation, love beats with the rhythm of God. I ask that my heart may be softened, that I may receive—receive God's love, receive love from others, receive miracles—and in the receiving, alchemize them, as the physical heart receives the blood in and alchemizes it to become new and pumps it back through the body; may my spiritual heart alchemize the love that I feel into the love that I give, that I become the one who siphons God's love here and now and gives it to humanity—wrapping my heart.

I breathe in, and I breathe out.

I ask that Christ may bless my back heart, that the back heart may be washed with the blessing of mercy that mercy may heal me—heal the bitterness, the pain, the cynicism, the rage, the old wounds, the rejection, the betrayal, all the wounds that I have held. I ask that Christ may clear it to the edges and the corners, the attics of my back heart. I ask that Christ may wash it first and cleanse it with the blessing of mercy, and that the law of forgiveness may be activated; and I ask that I may be blessed with forgiveness—forgiveness of others and forgiveness of myself, forgiveness of God, forgiveness in whole. And I ask that the Divine Mother may place Her hand on my back heart, for She is the seed of unconditional love, and I ask that She pulse this unconditional love through the back heart—allowing the back heart to find peace and rest in this unconditional love, that I may be swaddled from the crown to the tips of my toes in a love that holds me in the deepest safety, a love that loves every mistake I've made, a love that loves everything that I am; that I may be—and in the being, that I am love.

Transfiguration

I breathe in, and I breathe out.

I ask that Christ may bless my front solar plexus, that the front solar plexus may be seen, that I may witness all of the actions that I have taken, that I may witness myself for who I have become. And in the witnessing, I gain more energy, I gain more light, I gain more wonder—and it fuels my fire. In the witnessing of who I am and who I have become, my fire is fueled. In allowing God to witness me and allowing myself to see how God sees me, I am blessed with more energy to take the actions that are needed next that I may walk at the stride of God; for whatever I am inspired to do, I take action, and I do—but not alone. I take action with the power that is sourced from God. And I ask that a blessing may be placed upon my front solar plexus, that my actions are fueled by faith, not fear—by trust and belief.

I breathe in, and I breathe out.

I ask that Christ may bless my back solar plexus. I ask that Christ may go within my back solar plexus and gather in all the slime of fear, all of the clingy energy of victimhood, all of the terror, doubt and abuse that has been plaguing the very system of my body, and I ask that it may be gathered in from the very corners and edges of my being—and that Christ may hold them with love, that Christ may transfigure them into the truth of who I am; that the queen may arise; that I may be made whole here and now. I ask that the gifts of alchemy that I have been bestowed with may arise; that every time fear appears, I alchemize it into faith; every time doubt rises, I may breathe belief into existence; that I am the weaver of miracles, and that I am the one. I am the one.

For when I speak, the mountains move; for when I walk, the paths unfold. Faith is a rhythm that lives within me; miracles are wrapped around the very feet of my body, so each time I step, I become one with God.

I breathe in, and I breathe out.

I ask that Christ may bless my navel chakra, and in sacred submission, I hand over my will. I hand over my desires. I hand over my dreams. I hand over everything I want, and I ask You, God—may the highest good be done, whether it is that my dreams become realized or something greater is given. But I submit my will into God. And I surrender all of my fears and all of my suffering and all of my anxiety and overwhelm and terror and doubt—I surrender it into You, God—and ask that all of these attachments may be severed and shattered and that I may plug into You, God: that I may plug into the higher viewpoint, that I may plug into the higher will, that I may plug into the frequency that is God; that in this space, we become one.

I breathe in, and I breathe out.

I ask that Christ may bless my sacral chakra. I ask that Christ will go within my sacral chakra and, with the magnet of love, gather in all the shame—the shame for past mistakes, the shame of self-hate, the shame of self-loathing, the shame of self-criticism, the shame of not being good enough, the shame of not taking actions when called—all of the shame that has found its way within the very portal of creation, that God's love may magnetize it into a space that is held by Christ. And as it is held, it dissipates, and all that is left is a golden nugget of love—a love that is so rich, a love that is so deep, a love that is for me—my love for me. May this love tremble through my being, reminding every organ, every cell, down to my DNA coding, that I love me, and that God loves me as I am; that in this space I partner with God, I rise as the co-creator of such divinity, I am the portal that God's visions move through to be actualized onto this planet; that I am the body that births the creations that God has weaved into the very fibers of my body.

I breathe in, and I breathe out.

Transfiguration

I ask that Christ may bless my root chakra. I ask that Christ may go within and sit with the lepers inside of me—with the ones who are homeless, the ones who lack, the ones who do not feel loved, the ones who fear that there is never enough money, the ones who tremble in terror of not being supported, of being alone. And I ask that Christ may sit with every one of them within me and hold them and bless them with love—and then remind them of what is true.

What is true is abundance: they are enough to be loved as they are; there is always enough money—*always;* there's always enough time—*always;* there's always enough love—*always;* there's always enough support—*always*—for this is the truth of God, and may it become the rod that holds me up; may it become the truth that stabilizes the very essence of who I am. I ask that abundance may ripple out to the very edges and corners of my body and to the very edges and corners of the universe, that I become one with God.

I breathe in, and I breathe out.

I ask that Christ may bless my arms and my hands, that they may be prepped and prepared to do the work that I have been called to do on this planet—to be God's hands, to love as God loves, to serve as God serves, to write as God writes, to build as God builds.

I ask that Christ may bless my feet, that they may be washed from all my past sins, from all of my past mistakes; and that they may be prepared to sit with God, to walk with God, to make manifest God's visions on earth; that my feet may be coated with the directions of where God would have me go, that my feet may lead me there, that my feet may guide me, that they may be wrapped in the love of Christ and blessed and prepared for the path ahead.

I breathe in, and I breathe out.

I now take my burdens, my stress, my worries, and my suffering, and I pick them up, and I put them into God, and I ask that God may transfigure them—that they will now match the miracles that God has for me.

I ask that Christ may touch my cells, so my cells may match the frequency of the vision that God has given me, that I may become that woman—the woman who I was called to be. I watch the cells move to face the vision, receiving new commands, receiving new orders that match this vision, the vision that I have been given.

I breathe in, and I breathe out.

Now that my cells have been coded with this blueprint—the blueprint of the vision that I have received—I ask that Christ will go within my DNA coding and pull out the DNA strand that has kept me from following this vision—that has kept me small, that has kept me hiding my gifts—and I ask that this strand may disintegrate, dissipate, and be gone. And now I ask that Christ may weave a DNA strand from His very coding—the strand that matches the frequency of God's vision for me, the strand that matches the frequency of the miracles that I have been called to perform—and I ask that Christ may now graft His code into my DNA code, **and I receive it.**

I take three breaths, allowing my body to become one with this grafting, that it may be seamless and whole.

Breathing in . . . out. And in . . . and out. And in . . . and out.

We seal this transfiguration blessing up with gratitude.

Thank you, thank you, thank you, God.

Transfiguration

And in this energy, and in this frequency, I come to sit at the foot of God to receive. I ask that this energy will be magnified, that it will be multiplied to unfold the miracles that I could not even imagine.

I ask that God, and Christ, and the Divine Mother may place Their hands on my head to give me a blessing—that I may receive the words that are for me today.

And now I open my palms, and I ask God: "What is the number one action that You would have me do today that will help me bring this vision to life?"

I listen, and I receive.

I ask my angels that they may help me take this action today and that they may walk with me, and I ask them to open up the pathways that will allow this vision to come to fruition, the pathways that will allow this vision to be brought forth into actualized, realized truth.

I take a deep breath in to seal this work up in the deepest gratitude.

Thank you, thank you, thank you, God. And in love, and in sacred devotion, this is complete.

III.

Identity & Calling Blessings

Blessing of the Prophetess

This is a blessing to awaken the prophetess / prophet within you.

—--

I bless my crown chakra that acceptance will be poured through my body, that I may be in the deepest acceptance of whom I have been called to become and of whom I am called to be.

I ask that Christ will bless my third eye, that I may use my gifts as God intended me to use them—as a prophetess, as one who sees, one who heals, one who leads, one who sits with God.

I ask that Christ will bless my eyes, that I may see as a prophetess, that I may see the visions, that I may see the truths, and that I may see as God sees.

I ask that Christ may bless my ears, that I may hear God, that I may hear the clearness and the clarity of God.

Transfiguration

I ask that Christ may bless my nose, that I may receive as the prophetess.

I ask that Christ may bless my lips, that I may speak as the prophetess, that I may speak the words that God has called me to speak, that I may speak boldly, that I may speak truthfully, that I may speak with love: that when I speak, the mountains will move; that when I speak, hearts will be softened; that when I speak, those who listen may know God for themselves.

I ask that Christ will bless my nervous system, that it may be wired and strengthened in and through the light of Christ, that I may be quickened to walk with Christ and God.

I ask that Christ may bless my throat chakra, that I may allow others to see me as a prophetess, that I may allow others to see me in my gifts, that I may allow others to witness the hand of God through me.

I ask that Christ will bless my heart, that I may love as God loves, that I may serve as God serves, that I may receive myself as the prophetess, that I may love myself as the prophetess I am.

I ask that Christ will bless my back heart, that I may forgive myself for rejecting the prophetess, that I may forgive myself for rejecting who I am, and that I may love myself in the deepest places. That I may love the prophetess that I am, that I may love what God has called me to be, that I may forgive myself for all the times that I have rejected my calling, that I may forgive myself for all the times that I have rejected God, that I may forgive myself for all the times that I have rejected my gifts, that I may love every part of me—the prophetess, the human, the miracles, the mistakes, the wonder, the doubt, the faith, the inaction, and the action.

May I love the whole.

Identity & Calling Blessings

I ask that Christ will bless my front solar plexus, that I may stand forth and take action as the prophetess, that I may rise and be Her, that my actions may be in alignment with God.

I ask that Christ will bless my back solar plexus, that I may release the victim—the victim to the call, the victim to the callings, the victim to God, the victim to the miracles, the victim to the fear, the victim to the doubt—that I may release all of this, that it has no place or part within me anymore, and I step forward as the prophetess who weaves miracles, who unfolds truth, who heals, who speaks and it is done.

I am her.

I ask that Christ will bless my navel chakra, that all of my attachments to how I think this is going to go, how I think it should go, all of my fears of attachments of how I don't want it to go, all of my attachments to this life, my expectations of what this life should be—I surrender in sacred submission to God.

I sacrifice my will for God's will.

I sacrifice my way for the higher way.

I ask that Christ will bless my sacral chakra, that I may love myself as God loves me, that I may love the prophetess as God loves her, that I may honor myself as God honors me.

I ask that Christ will bless my root chakra, that I may love abundance, that I may trust in the law of abundance, that as I stand in the power of God, I will live and breathe the law of abundance.

I claim abundance—abundance of love, abundance of miracles, abundance of finances, abundance of peace, abundance of joy, abundance of creation.

I claim them, and they are so because I am a prophetess.

Transfiguration

May it be done.

I cleanse my arms and my hands, that they may be the hands of a prophetess, that they may heal as a prophetess heals, that they may make whole as a prophetess makes whole, that they may love as a prophetess loves, that they may be God's hands through me.

I ask that Christ may bless my feet, that they will be cleansed, that in this moment I will be made new, that these feet will take me where God would take me.

Blessing of Self-Love

This is a blessing to awaken the deepest places of self-love within you.

—-

I ask that Christ will bless this water, that it will be cleansed and cleaned and activated down to the molecular structure—the molecular structure of miracles—that it may match miracles.

I ask that Christ will bless my crown chakra from the top of my head all the way down to the tips of my toes, that I may clear out any and all self-hate, that I may love myself as God loves me throughout every cell of my body, that I may love myself down to my DNA coding.

I ask that Christ will bless my third eye, that I may love my gifts as God loves my gifts, that I may love my gifts exactly as they are.

I ask that Christ will bless my eyes, that I may see myself as God sees me, that I may see myself in the deepest place of love as God sees me, as God loves me.

Identity & Calling Blessings

I ask that Christ will bless my ears, that I might hear God, that I may hear how much God loves me, that I may hear how wonderful I am, that I may hear how precious I am, that I may hear how known I am.

I ask that Christ will bless my nose, that I may receive. I may receive—receive love from myself. I may receive love from myself.

I ask that Christ will bless my lips, that I may love myself with my words, that I will only speak the words that are of love to myself, that all self-hate and all self-deprecation will be cleared out of my body completely and wholly, that I may speak the words to myself that God would speak to me, that whatever words come out of my mouth may be as if God was speaking to me with love.

I ask that Christ will bless my C-7, that my nervous system will be loved, that my nervous system will feel accepted just as I am, that I may love myself, be kind to myself, and listen to my body—do as my body needs.

I ask that Christ may bless my throat, that I may allow myself to see myself as God sees me—that I may see myself as God sees me through every minute, through every struggle, through every celebration, through every single thing—that I may see myself as God sees me, that I may hear myself as God hears me.

And I ask that Christ will bless the back of my head, that all the chatter and all the noise and all the loops of all the years—of not loving myself, the years of beating myself up, shaming myself, critiquing myself, tearing myself apart—that they may be dissolved, that in the ruins of this, of these patterns, the true truth arises: the truth that I love myself down to the very cells of my being.

I ask that Christ will bless my front heart, that I may love myself unconditionally—every part of my body, every part of my behavior,

Transfiguration

every part of my personality, every word I say, every action I do, every word I write, every mistake I make—that I love it all.

That I love myself as God loves me.

I ask that Christ will bless my back heart, that I may release all the bitterness, and all the hatred, and all the pain, and all the grief, and all the resentment, all the cynicism, and all of the rage, all of the pain, all of the times I have stomped my feet at life being unfair and God being unfair, and all the times that I have hated myself, despised myself, that they will be cleaned and cleansed and cleared from off of my body, that I may be in the deepest place of forgiveness with myself.

I forgive myself. I forgive myself. I forgive myself. I forgive myself. I forgive myself. I forgive myself. I forgive myself.

For all the mistakes. For all the decisions I made. I forgive myself for every time I have not listened to my knowingness. I forgive myself for every time I have not held my boundaries. And I forgive myself as God forgives me.

I ask that Christ will bless my front solar plexus. I ask that I will take action as God takes action. I ask that I may take action toward loving myself.

I ask that Christ will bless my back solar plexus. I ask that Christ will go within my back solar plexus and gather in all the negative entities and negative energies, the familial generational patterns that are stuck within my back solar plexus: everything that creates so much victim energy—victim energy to my self-hate, victim energy to my self-deprecation, victim energy to not ever being loved.

I ask that Christ will gather all these in—all of these parts—and wrap them in love, that they may know true love, and that within that love

Identity & Calling Blessings

they may rise and become love, awakening the queen, the alchemist, and the one who is loved.

I ask that Christ will touch my back solar plexus to wake up the alchemist who can take the darkness and turn it into light, who can take the self-hate and turn it into self-love, who can take all this pain and turn it into the fertilizer for the most beautiful growth of love—that I may love myself as God loves me.

I ask that Christ will bless my navel chakra, that I may release all of my attachments of self-hate, all of the whatever I get—whatever rewards I'm getting for the self-hate—I release. I release my attachments to them.

Instead, I plug into Christ. I attach myself to love. I ask that I may love every part of me. *I ask that I may love every part of me.*

I ask that Christ will bless my sacral chakra, that I may release all the shame—the shame that has tried to drown me, the shame of bad decisions, the shame of every time I haven't listened to my knowingness, the shame of every time I've listened to the hungers of my body and not my truth, the shame of all the self-hate that has attacked my body, through all the abuse that I went through and all the self-hate that came from that abuse—from not being able to protect myself, from not being able to hold boundaries for myself.

All of the shame that has grown in the darkest corners of my sacral chakra—I ask that Christ will clear it out, that Christ will pour love through my body, that I may have love in my body, that I may love myself as God loves me.

I ask that God may help me love myself as God loves me. Help me to be of one mind and one heart with God—that I may love myself.

Transfiguration

I ask that Christ will bless my root chakra, that I may be in the deepest place of love, that I may love abundance. I may have an abundance of love. An abundance of love. An abundance of love.

I ask that Christ will bless my arms and my hands, that my hands may be of love today, that they may love myself, that they may treat myself with so much love.

I ask that Christ will bless my feet, that my feet may be God's feet, that I may walk with love today in all that I do. *That I may walk in love today.*

I take this burden of self-hate. I take the burden of self-deprecation. I take the burden of self-loathing. I take the burden of self-criticism. I take the burden of just self-disgust and self-hate—and I take these burdens and I place them into God.

I place them into God.

With Christ's help—because this one needs Christ's help. I ask that Christ will help me lift these burdens and place them into God with me.

I ask that God will alchemize them into love—that God can even take this darkness and turn it into love.

I ask that Christ will touch my cells so that they may match the frequency of self-love, that the blueprint of divine love may be placed within the very nucleus of my cells.

I then ask that Christ will go within my DNA coding and pull out the code of self-hate that will disintegrate and dissolve within the presence of Christ.

I release this code, as it no longer serves me.

Identity & Calling Blessings

I ask that Christ will graft a code of Christ's DNA coding into my DNA: the thread of deep, self-love. I ask that this divine code may transfer with ease into my DNA strands and become one with me.

I ask that God, Christ, and the Divine Mother seal this work up with a blessing. I ask that They place Their hands on my head to give me a blessing, that I may receive a blessing of shifting my energy into self-love.

That this blessing may begin the catalyst toward a life of deep, profound self-love.

Then I ask for words that I need to hear today—that will lead me, that will guide me, that will teach me.

Thank you, thank you, thank you.

—-

I Am Loved Blessing

This is a blessing to clear out the fear of not being loved and awaken the truth that you are loved.

—-

I ask that Christ touch the walls, the ceilings, the floors, the doors, the windows, the beds—anything and everything in this room—that it will be cleaned, cleansed, and cleared, and then activated to the highest vibrational frequency, the frequency of miracles.

I ask that light may cleanse me from the crown of my head down to the tips of my toes, clearing out my inner column, clearing out anything and everything that I don't want to be a magnet in my body,

Transfiguration

clearing out anything and everything that says I'm not supported, that I'm alone, that I don't belong, that I am rejected.

I ask that Christ will clear this out of my center column, that these will no longer be magnets in my life.

I ask that my center column will be activated in the deepest places of being received.

I am received.
I am received.
I am received.
I am received.

That this is what awakens within my center column: I am received. I am whole. I am loved.

I am received. I am received. I am received.

I am lovable. I am loved. I am wanted.

I am lovable, I am loved, and I am wanted.

I ask that all of these would be what makes up my center column.

Let these become the magnets inside of me.

I ask that Christ will bless this water, that it may be cleaned and cleansed and cleared and activated to the highest vibrational frequency.

I ask that God will bless my crown chakra, from the top of my head down to the tips of my toes, cleaning me out completely.

I ask that Christ will bless my third eye, that I have access to my spiritual gifts, that I may see as God sees today.

Identity & Calling Blessings

I ask that Christ will bless my eyes, that I may see all the places and times that I have been received, that I may see all the places and times that I am loved, that I am wanted; that I may see the truth—that I am received, that I am loved, and that I am wanted.

I ask that Christ will bless my third eye, that I may use my gifts, that I may use them in a way that allows me to feel received by myself, that I will receive my own gifts, that by receiving my gifts, by loving my gifts, I am allowing myself to feel seen, received, and loved.

I ask that Christ will bless my crown chakra, that it may completely clear my body of anything and everything that says I am not loved, I am always rejected, I am never received, I am not wanted—clearing it out completely, that it never has a place or part within me again.

That whatever Velcro has attached those feelings, thoughts, attachments to me—they are released, that the stickiness is gone, that the law of non-resistance may be poured through my being, never to attach to those again.

I ask that Christ will bless my nose, that I may be able to receive, that I may be able to receive being received, that I may be received, that I may receive me.

I ask that Christ will bless my ears, that I may hear: that I may hear God, that I may hear that God receives me, that I may hear that God loves me, that I may hear that I am wanted by God, that I may hear the calling that God has given me.

I ask that Christ will bless my lips, that I may speak as God speaks—meaning I speak the words that receive me, that I say the words that I receive me, that I say the words that prove that I love me, that I say the words that prove that I want me, activating the magnet of being received within my body by the very words that I speak.

Transfiguration

I ask that Christ will bless my throat, that it may be cleaned and cleansed and cleared, that it may be activated, that I may allow myself to see myself as God sees me, that I may allow myself to want myself as God wants me, that I may allow others to see me as God sees me, that I may allow others to desire and want me as God does, that I may free my voice—holding nothing back, no borders, no barriers—full expression, full expansion, full love, full light, full wonder.

I ask that Christ will bless the back of my head, to release all the loops, that Christ will touch the loops—the loops that I loop in, in my mind—that say I am not loved, I am not wanted, I am not received, I am always rejected.

That Christ may touch these loops, that they no longer become loops, that they no longer are loops, but that they are freed, that they are cleared, that they have been made into new—into a new line, not a loop—a line, a line of truth.

The truth is that I have always been wanted, and I have always been received, and I am never rejected, for I am a queen, and I walk with God, and so I am received.

This is the truth that I plant into my subconscious mind.

I ask that Christ will bless C-7, healing my nervous system, healing my nervous system, healing my nervous system—that it may be cleaned, that it may be cleared, that it may be cleansed, that it may match the frequency of God. That it may match the frequency of God.

God does not need to be received or wanted and is always rejected by many. It never changes that it is God. It never changes the fact that it is God.

Identity & Calling Blessings

Allowing this truth to be within me—that if I am not wanted, or not received, or if I am rejected, it does not change the consistency of who I am. It does not change the consistency of the god I am.

Letting that run through the very electrical current that is within my nervous system.

I ask that Christ will bless my front heart, that I may love myself as God loves me, that I may receive myself as God receives me, that I may give as God gives—without any attachment to being received or loved or wanted—that I may give solely from the deepest place of pure love to give.

I ask that Christ will bless my back heart, that I will forgive all of those who have rejected me, that I will forgive all of those who did not want me or love me; I will forgive all of those who could not receive me.

I forgive them, for they know not what they do. For they reject, and they do not love, and they cannot receive—simply because they reject and do not love and cannot receive themselves.

And so in my deepest compassion, I wrap them in love and forgiveness.

And I forgive all the parts inside of me who have rejected me, all the parts inside of me who do not love me, and all the parts inside of me who cannot receive me as I am, who want to change me, who want me to be different, who want me to conform, who want me to look different, to act different.

I forgive these parts, for they know not what they do. They have just been here because they were passed down from generation upon generation.

And so I release them of their jobs today, and I forgive them in love.

Transfiguration

I ask that Christ will bless my front solar plexus, that I will take action today, that I will take action that is rooted in the deepest place of acceptance of who I am, that I will take action in the deepest place of love of who I am, that I may walk with God today.

I ask that Christ will bless my back solar plexus, that I will forgive and release all of the victim energy—all the victim energy of being victim to not being loved, being victim to not being wanted, being victim to being rejected over and over again.

I release these, as they are not true. I release them, as they are no longer needed to participate with me.

I release all of the doubt in myself. I release all of the doubt in people loving me. I release all of the doubt that people can receive me and want me. I release the doubt that has brewed because of my experiences with rejection.

May they be cleared. May they be cleansed. May they have no part here anymore. And I thank them for their participation. And may they now be gone.

And I activate within my back solar plexus the deepest place of faith, the deepest place of wonder, the deepest place of belief, the deepest place of creation—that I claim the queen that I am, that I claim the goddess that I am, that I claim the prophetess that I am.

That I am. That I am.

I ask that Christ will bless my navel chakra, that it may be cleaned and cleansed, that all of my attachments to being rejected, all of my attachments to being unwanted, all of my attachments to being unlovable may be cleaned and cleansed and cleared. May be cleaned and cleansed and cleared.

Identity & Calling Blessings

That I may be in the deepest place of sacred surrender, handing over all of these attachments to God and allowing myself to be only attached into God—the Divine Light, the Divine Presence, the Divine Essence—pure peace, pure wonder, pure love, pure acceptance, pure divinity, pure unadulterated acceptance of who I am.

I ask that Christ will bless my sacral chakra, that I may release all shame, that I may release all the shame that I've had for being who I am, all the shame that I have felt for being rejected, all of the shame for not being wanted, not being loved, not being received or accepted.

I release all this shame, as it has no place or part here anymore.

May it detach from my very essence and from the core central column of my being.

May it be cleaned, cleansed, cleared, and gone—activating the deepest place of self-love within my sacral chakra.

Activating the truest form of self-love, which is absolute divine creation. Activating the truest place of self-love, which is to love every part of me, to accept every piece of me, to want every part of me.

I ask that Christ will bless my root chakra, that it may be filled with the most absolute divine abundance—abundance of love, abundance of wonder, abundance of truth, abundance of being loved, abundance of being received, abundance of being wanted, abundance of this.

I am loved. I am wanted. I am lovable.

I am received as I am. I am wanted as I am. I am loved as I am. As I am. As I am.

Here and now, I always have been. I always will be. For I am a goddess, and I claim that.

Transfiguration

I ask that God will bless my hands, that they may be God's hands, that they may love and receive and want me, that I may serve as God serves.

I ask that Christ will bless my feet, that my feet may be cleaned and cleansed and cleared, that I may stand as who I have been called to be, that I may stand in the deepest place of assurance and claiming—claiming my gifts, claiming my purpose, claiming my calling, walking with God.

May this be so now.

I ask that all these parts inside of me that have been rejected from my earliest ages, that have felt unlovable—everything, every moment, every time, every example of when I was rejected, not lovable, not wanted—I'm going to pick them all up. I'm going to place them into God.

I'm going to ask that God will transmute them and transform them, transfigure them into light, transform them into: I am loved, I am lovable, I am received, I am made whole in this love.

I ask that Christ may touch my cells so that they may be awakened and enlivened with love. I ask that the blueprint of deep, profound, unconditional love will be placed into the nucleus of each cell within my body, that they become one with this new order and arise in this new pattern.

I ask that my cells match the frequency of God, that through this blessing my cells may transform to match the frequency of being loved, of being wanted, of being received.

That this becomes a new blueprint that my cells follow.

Identity & Calling Blessings

That this becomes a blueprint not only for me but for my whole generational line below me.

That this becomes our new truth.

I ask that Christ will go within my DNA coding and pull out the strand of not being loved or chosen and dissolve it so that it may be obsolete and complete. I then ask that Christ will take a DNA strand from His code: the strand of unconditional love, and to know and feel that I am chosen.

I breathe in this graft that it may become complete and whole, that my body may receive it with ease and peace.

And I ask that God and the Divine Mother and Christ will come and place Their hands on my head and give me a blessing—that I may receive the words that I need to hear today, and that in this blessing, I may hear the words my cells need to receive.

Thank you, thank you, thank you.

———

IV.

Abundance & Divine Mother Blessings

Blessing with the Divine Mother around Abundance

This is a blessing that allows you to work with the Divine Mother and awaken abundance.

We are going to ask that God will pour light through our bodies, all the way down, out of the palms of our hands into the water, to clean it and to cleanse it and to clear it—and that it may be transformed all the way down to a molecular structure, the molecular structure of miracles.

We're going to take the water; and we're going to bless our crown chakras.

We're going to ask that today, the Divine Mother will bless our crown chakras, that we may be healed from the tops of our heads all the way down to the soles of our feet, and that Her love may dissipate all lack

Abundance & Divine Mother Blessings

from within our bodies, that it will have no place or part within us anymore.

We're going to bless our third eyes. We're going to ask that the Divine Mother may place Her hands on our third eyes so that we may use the abundance of our gifts not just sparingly—like thinking that we can only use them a little bit, that we don't want to overuse them, that we don't want to run out.

There's never an end to our gifts—ever. There's never an end to our ability to give. There's never an end to the amount of magic that we have. There's never an end to the amount of magic that we *can* have.

There's more than enough time. There's more than enough money. There's more than enough peace. There's more than enough love—just like those moments that we had as mothers in the middle of the night, rocking our babies, and the world stopped. There were no other kids to take care of. There were no bills to pay. There were no husbands to please. There were no clothes to fold. There was just you and this baby. And that's when She was with us. And She says, "Come rock. I know that there's just always enough."

So we're going to bless our third eyes so that *that* becomes our truth. And if we look at the physiological portion of our body, the third eye is a gland—the pineal gland—and the pineal gland is actually what gives our cells commands. And so when we bless our third eye, our pineal gland, with this blessing of "there's always more than enough," then that is the order our pineal gland—the commander—gives our cells.

And so we're going to ask for the pineal gland to be the commander like this—that our pineal glands may command our cellular blueprints to follow the blueprint that there is always enough. We're going to breathe that in.

Transfiguration

We are going to ask that the Divine Mother may cleanse our noses, that we may receive abundance—abundance of wonder, abundance of wisdom, abundance of brilliance, abundance of finances, abundance of money flowing in from every edge and corner—

Just as there's always an abundance of oxygen for us to breathe. There's always enough grass.

If you were to pull out one blade of grass, it wouldn't affect the land; it wouldn't affect the greenery. Even a thousand blades of grass wouldn't touch it. That feeling of, no matter how much you use, no matter how many times you pray, no matter how much you ask God, it doesn't make a dent: let that move into your truth and into your being.

It never makes a dent for God. There's always more than enough—more than enough prayers, more than enough asks, more than enough time sitting with God, more than enough requests—there's just *enough*. You can ask as many times as you want; it wouldn't make a dent. I want you to breathe that in . . .

And now we're going to bless our ears. We're going to ask that Christ and the Divine Mother will cleanse our ears, that our ears may be unclogged so that they can be tuned to the frequency of the voice of God—so that we may hear God's voice, that we may hear our Divine Mother's voice, that we may hear Christ. We may hear these messages that are for us—*then* are for us to give to the world.

We're going to bless the back of the head, and we're going to ask that the Divine Mother may touch the back of the head, and in Her unconditional love, She shows us all the loops we've been living in—and She shows it to us with love, like the little kid who keeps putting their shoes on the wrong feet.

It's the same energy of Her looking at our loops—our stories, the ones we keep getting stuck in—and we want to shame ourselves, like, "Ah, why do I keep getting stuck in this loop? Why do we keep getting stuck in this loop?" And She's like, "Hey, your shoes just go on the other foot. . . . Hey, this is just a loop that you were given. It's okay." **But we can change it.**

I want you to feel Her love come in—and it's Her love that changes the loops because She just took the time. She's going to rewire them for us.

She says, "Honey, it's okay. I'm just going to change these for you. You didn't have time to put your shoes on the right feet. You didn't care because you had so much going on. But right now, I'll re-wire it."

I want you to allow Her to rewire the loops inside of you—the ones that have always said, "I don't deserve it. I'm not enough. I'm never enough. No matter what I do, it's not enough. I don't know how to have abundance. I'm afraid of abundance. I won't keep it; it will leave like it always has. It won't stay. I'm married to fear instead of faith."

We're going to ask for Her to go in—and any other loop that we can't see—we're going to ask Her to rewire them so that the truth lives within us: the truth of abundance, the truth that we have always been deserving of abundance. The truth is that we **are** love, no matter how many mistakes we've made. The truth is that we are enough just for being here—for just breathing. **We're enough.**

Breathe that in.

Breathe that out.

We're going to now bless the nervous system.

Transfiguration

We're going to ask that our nervous systems be rewired to match the frequency of abundance—because our nervous systems have been wired to match the frequency of lack, and that's what it knows. So we're going to ask that our nervous system will match the frequency of abundance, and that it may feel comfortable in abundance, and that it may feel comfortable in receiving abundance—abundance of finances, abundance of love, abundance of joy, abundance of wonder, abundance of peace.

One more breath in—just letting it reset—kind of like when you take your modem apart and then you put it back together: it just needs a 30-second reset and then it's back online.

Now we're going to bless our lips.

We're going to ask that the Divine Mother may cleanse our lips, that our lips may be cleaned and cleansed, cleared and anointed, that we speak only abundance, that abundance is the only word that comes out of our mouths, and that we may build the worlds—that we build the worlds in which we want to live. And that our lips may be cleansed and anointed before we meet with God.

Now we bless our throats. And we're going to ask that the Divine Mother may cleanse our throats in love and compassion and mercy; that She may free us from the ropes of bondage—the things that have clasped us, the ropes that have clasped us to our prisons: the prisons of silence, the prisons of being ignored, the prisons of not being seen, the prisons of people not saying yes, the prisons of being alone.

We ask that She clean those out—and in their place, put us in the corridors of the castle: the castle of freedom, the large hallways of liberation, the queendom—the place where we get to stand and reign; the place where we get to speak and be heard; the place where we get to speak and be seen; the place where we get to speak and impact in safety and protection and liberation.

Now breathe in.

We are going to bless our front hearts. We're going to ask the Divine Mother to place the palms of Her hands on our front hearts so the rhythm of Her heartbeat and the rhythm of our heartbeat become one; that Her love moves through our hearts, and as Her love moves through our hearts, Her love moves out of our hearts and that we become like a direct siphon to bring Her heart through our hearts into the world.

And as we siphon Her love through, it heals our unmothered hearts.

And whatever leftover brokenness that says our mothers couldn't love us enough, that there just wasn't enough love for us—that lie is gone, because now we feel that with every breath we can bring in the Divine Mother's love, and it is a love that has no condition.

You do not have to earn this love.

You do not have to be good enough for this love.

You don't have to be beautiful enough for this love. You don't have to be perfect enough for this love. You don't have to do what's right for this love. She just gives it to you. It's just love. It's just given, and it's given, and it's given.

Breathe that in.

We're going to bless our back hearts, and we're going to ask that the Divine Mother may wash our back hearts with the law of mercy. It's like the mercy that we give—the mercy of when our children make big mistakes, how we just hold them in our arms and we let them know: this doesn't change how we love you. Welcome to humanity. A

Transfiguration

blessing of mercy is poured over them—and similarly now allows **you** to have that same blessing of mercy from the Divine Mother, allowing it to disperse through you.

And as Her mercy runs through you, bitterness is gone, cynicism is gone, resentment is gone.

For in Her love they cannot exist. They're like bacteria that, as soon as bleach touches it, is nonexistent—it can't exist. When Her love appears, bitterness can't exist, resentment can't exist, cynicism can't exist. I want you to breathe that in—and feel them cleaned out of your body, all the way gone.

Now we're going to bless our front solar plexus. We're going to ask the Divine Mother to bless our front solar plexus. She wants me to call it the "solar center," and then She keeps showing me the sun—like a solar disk.

It's like She's showing me the sun is in your front solar plexus. And when you activate the sun in this space of the body, stagnation can't exist; procrastination doesn't exist. The sun doesn't halfway shine—ever. The sun doesn't have a dimmer. It doesn't have bad days where it's like, "I can only shine at 50% today." And I know this because I lived in Arizona, where there's never a cloud—ever.

I am shown that the sun has never *not* shined—it's always there. Here we get clouds, and sometimes it feels like there's a dimmer, but the sun never does not shine. And so, allowing that blessing to be on our front solar plexus—claiming that we own the sun inside of us—what that does is negate all of the old lies: "I don't have enough energy for that. I don't have the bandwidth for that. I don't have the capacity for that." All of those are lies—because we are the sun.

And so we're going to place that within us as the truth that has always been the truth—but no one told us until now.

Abundance & Divine Mother Blessings

Breathe that in.

We are going to bless our back solar plexus, and we're going to ask the Divine Mother—so I'm shown an image of, for example, there are two ways this goes. A little kid accidentally knocks over the vase and it crashes everywhere, and the mother comes in and screams and yells. The little kid is just so sorry; they didn't mean to—but it's devastating for them, and then they just walk away being like, *"No, I can't do it right. I just can't."*

And then the Divine Mother shows this version of a little kid cartwheeling in the front room and accidentally hitting the vase—because their cartwheels aren't quite right, not yet. The glass goes everywhere; the Divine Mother comes in with a smile on Her face and gloves for them both and says, "Hey, how many pieces can you pick up in ten minutes? I bet I can win."

And in that moment, the love that this child feels seeps out of every pore of their body. The Divine Mother says, "This is what needs to go into the back solar plexus—for every moment you felt you were a victim; for every moment you felt you weren't good enough; for every moment you felt you didn't deserve to be loved, that you couldn't do it right." The Divine Mother says, "Hey, that cartwheel's almost there. Next time let's go do it in the grass together. Right now, I bet I can beat you in picking up the glass."

And a game is made, and love is poured, and mercy is offered. And as we breathe that into our back solar plexus, it wakes up the peace; it wakes up the abundance; it wakes up the love that loves and loves and loves and loves—*no matter what.*

You're going to breathe it in, and you're going to breathe it out.

And now we're going to bless our navel chakra. We're going to ask the Divine Mother—and we bless our navel chakras. She shows me

Transfiguration

the umbilical cord attached to our own mothers and how it had been fed with lack because no one had loved them; that's why they couldn't love us. And She takes the umbilical cord and attaches it to Her and says, "You will forever be nourished now. You will be forever loved now—for here and evermore."

And that true lineage of who you are is reinstated and restored now—a true priestess of the Divine Mother, a true queen of divinity and abundance, one whose love fills all. A rebirth is now.

We're now going to bless our sacral chakra.

We're going to ask the Divine Mother that She may place Her hands on our womb, that Her love will clear out all shame: all the shame that wasn't even ours to begin with—all the shame for not doing things right, for not being enough, for not being good enough, for not fitting the patterns, for not fitting the rules, for not being quiet enough, for not being perfect enough—all the shame for every mistake made.

And instead, Her pouring Her love through us—watching this love move from the sacral chakra up—and it starts to swirl like golden honey throughout every part of the body, letting every organ know that it IS enough; letting every bone know that it IS enough; letting every cell know that it IS enough; letting the very DNA coding within know that it IS enough; letting you know that you are enough—just as you are.

That you are enough—just as you are.

She is showing me this well.

There's a well at the top of this hill in Japan, and every morning I would walk up this hill. I'd walk up this mountain—up the steps, hundreds of steps—every day I would walk up this to get to the top of the mountain to pray. At this well, the water would start to go down,

Abundance & Divine Mother Blessings

and then all of a sudden it would just magically rise to the top, and it would overflow. And there was something—that God would meet me every day and show me how this well remained full.

For it never emptied. And not only did it refill, but it flooded—it flooded over onto the rocks so much that there was moss that just grew abundantly, even though no one was ever there. It was just me and this well and this water. And She showed me the well just now, and She said, "This is what happens in your sacral chakra: the love will never deplete. This love pours in from Me to you—from God to you—so that it never depletes; it never runs out. Your creations never run out. Your magic never runs out. Your self-love never runs out. Your ability to create with God never runs out. It's the well that always flows."

Breathe that in and allow that to be true.

We're going to bless the root chakra, and we're going to ask the Divine Mother to pour Her love into the root chakra—and it is a love that is the deepest rooted safety. It is a ground that never shakes; it is a ground that never can break; it is a ground that never lets you fall. It is the deepest of warmth, and it is the support of abundance.

And She's showing me a weave—there's a certain type of weave; it's interesting. It's almost like silk. And She shows me how silk is made from these silkworms, and that the way that it is woven together creates it to be the strongest weave. And it's the lightest fabric you can find, but when you place it on your body, it holds in heat.

She's saying that's what She wants us to feel in the root chakra: it's so natural, like from the soft silkworm—it's this natural fabric; it's natural, and it's woven so tightly that it's almost impossible to tear, and it's so light, and it's so warm, and it's everything. That's what She's saying in the root chakra—*let it be easy.*

All of the abundance—let it be easy.

Transfiguration

Let it protect you. Let it be light. Let it be natural. Let it be soft. Let it be beautiful. Let it be all.

We're going to breathe that in. We're going to breathe it out.

Then we're going to bless our arms and our hands, and we're going to ask that they may be anointed to be the Divine Mother's hands on this earth—that our hands may serve as the Divine Mother; that our hands may hold as the Divine Mother; that our hands may caress as the Divine Mother; that our hands may swaddle as the Divine Mother. She says, "Let Me bless others, through you."

We're going to bless our feet.

We're going to ask specifically that Christ will come in and wash our feet—that we will be prepared for the path ahead, and that we will walk as the Divine Mother; that we will be walking pathways that look dead, but as we walk, flowers are born, beauty is awakened, life is restored.

We bless that our very presence on this planet is the breath of abundance.

Now we're going to pick up whatever lack is left—whatever generational patterns of lack that have been left within our bodies: any patterns of not deserving abundance, any patterns of fear that abundance is coming and that it will be ripped out from within us, any patterns that say, "I'm not good enough," and any other patterns that have been attached to lack—we're going to pick them up in the palms of our hands, and we're going to put them into God.

We're going to ask that they be transfigured, that they will match the frequency of abundance, that they will match the frequency of the Divine Mother.

Abundance & Divine Mother Blessings

And then we're going to ask that Christ—who's the greatest alchemist of all—touch our cells, that our cells may match the blueprint of the Divine Mother. We're going to watch our cells move to know this blueprint, knowing that when we activate the blueprint of the Divine Mother, we are abundant.

And as we are abundance, abundance matches in. And in this frequency, we come to say, "It is finished."

So we ask to humbly sit at the foot of God. And we ask for a healing to take place. We ask that Christ will go within our bodies and find the strand—the DNA strand—that was given to us that has been living out the patterns of our life: the DNA strand of not deserving, not enough; the DNA strand that has attracted in lack; the one that says "not worthy."

I ask that Christ will take it out of our DNA, and as it leaves our bodies, it disintegrates from the presence of Christ. And then we ask that Christ will take His DNA coding and graft it into our DNA codes—the one that is the Divine Mother's code, the one that He carries within Him. We ask for this graft to take place here and now.

May we be blessed to be the one who is loved just as we are; the one worthy enough as we are; deserving because we are breathing; the one that is wrapped, initiated, and soaked in the Divine Mother's love and presence—and that it may be placed within us.

As you do this next out-breath, bring it down into the body, allowing it to find its place within you—breathing with the new rhythm, the Divine Mother's code within: the code of abundance, the code of abundance of love, abundance of peace, abundance of finances, abundance of safety, abundance of comfort.

We ask that this blessing today—this grafting of codes, this healing—will be sealed with a blessing.

Transfiguration

We ask that God, the Divine Mother, and Christ will place Their hands on our heads to give us a blessing, that we may receive the words that are for us today. And so we seal this blessing from the crown of our heads to the tips of our toes, in the deepest, deepest places of gratitude.

Thank you, thank you, thank you, God.

—-

If you have made it here, *take a moment to sit with me.*

This is not a book meant to be read once and then discarded. It was never intended to be a two-dimensional experience. Transfiguration is full-bodied—mind, heart, soul, and divinity unified as one.

Return to these pages when you need to remember: *Remember that you are not alone. Remember that you are a steward of God's work. Remember that you are a free agent.*

You are the one who chooses.

You choose to ask.
You choose to listen
You choose to do.

You choose how you feel before the calling is given. You choose how you feel in the middle of the pressure and the intensity. And you choose how you feel once you have crossed to the other side of the vision.

Return often.
To your own prayer corner.
To sit at the foot of God.

And live as the prophet who speaks with the Supreme Being—the One who knows you, loves you, *and is grateful that you have said yes.*

-Keira

Made in the USA
Coppell, TX
24 February 2026